CELESTINE SIBLEY

A Granddaughter's Reminiscence

Jan. 15, 2008

For Marianne,

With all good blessings —

Sibley

Celestine Sibley

A Granddaughter's Reminiscence

Celestine Sibley Fleming

d

HILL STREET PRESS
Athens, Georgia

A HILL STREET PRESS BOOK

Published in the United States of America by
Hill Street Press LLC
191 East Broad Street, Suite 209
Athens, Georgia 30601-2848 USA
706-613-7200
info@hillstreetpress.com
www.hillstreetpress.com

Hill Street Press is committed to preserving the written word.
Every effort is made to print books on acid-free paper
with a significant amount of post-consumer recycled content.

Text and cover design by Anne Richmond Boston.

Printed in the United States of America.

ISBN # 1-892514-68-0

10   9   8   7   6   5   4   3   2   1

First printing

Library of Congress Cataloging-in-Publication Data

Fleming, Sibley.
    Celestine Sibley : a granddaughter's reminiscence / by Celestine
Sibley Fleming.
        p.   cm.
    ISBN 1-892514-68-0 (alk. paper)
    1. Sibley, Celestine. 2. Novelists, American—20th century—Biography.
3. Women authors, American—Family relationships. 4. Journalists—United
States—Biography. 5. Grandmothers—Georgia—Biography. 6. Georgia—
Social life and customs. I. Title.
    PS3569.I256 Z67   2000
    813' .54—dc21
    [B]   99-087287

To 'Tine with love, Tibo

INTRODUCTION

They tell me it's grief. A found possession—shoes, old loafers, loaded into the back of my station wagon from the boat—the boat that carried *her* back across to the shore. I slip out of my own shoes to try on the battered shoes and cut my bare feet on the oyster shells on the shore. I step into them one at a time and they fit because 'Tine and me were both a perfect size ten, just like Jackie O. The shoes feel good though they are worn, perhaps because they are worn. They make a sound like sandpaper on wood as I shuffle across the parking lot, trying to get my mind around the thing—*'Tine is gone.*

When my grandmother, Celestine Sibley, died on August 15, 1999, the papers were filled with stories about her professional life as a reporter and author, what she'd meant to millions of readers, to her home state of Georgia, and to the passing of an era. Georgia Governor Roy Barnes made a public statement and for a whole week, she was mourned on the nightly news. Her life as a Southern icon was laid out for all to see.

✂ Jill Smith, an old-time bookseller who often accompanied my grandmother to signings, called weeks after all of the publicity had died down to see how I was doing.

I said the expected, "I miss her."

"I do too," she agreed. "It's strange, but I especially miss her in the mornings with my first cup of coffee."

"The mornings!" I sighed. "That's true. I miss her so much in the mornings—my brother was telling me how he missed talking to her on his cell phone when he drove to work. That's when we all talked, in the morning. Now that she's gone, the phone doesn't seem to ring anymore. Or, if it does, there's no reason to hurry and answer it."

"That's a little different from how I feel," Jill said thoughtfully, "I didn't *talk* to her every morning—I read her, but it was *like* talking to her."

✂ My little sister Betsy was just thirteen years old when 'Tine died. She wrote a poem to express her feelings of loss.

My Grandmother, the Magician
by
Mary Everitt Elizabeth Vance
a.k.a. Betsy

I once knew this lady who was my best friend
She was a great magician known around the land
Whenever I was down or feeling sad
She would take out her wand and magic hat
She would sit me down and with a wink of an eye
Perform a trick so secret and sly

She was a magician of sorts—
A special kind
She could calm your heart and ease your mind
She could make wonders happen—
Or just small things.
No matter the trick,
She could make your heart sing.

In an instant everything would be alright
Then I would run up and hug her tight.
To me her powers were ongoing and endless.
I never thought that she would have to rest.
Over time, though, she lost her magic way.
She would get weaker and weaker every day.

I hated to see it happen, to see her go.
Magicians can't stop, can't stop the show.
Her time was here and though she was great,
Her powers had ended and she had reached her fate.
I miss her so much but its good to say
I will see her again someday
Until then I will fill her shoes as best I can
I want her to know I'm her biggest fan.

Because of my relationship to 'Tine, this book isn't so much about Celestine Sibley, the public figure, as it is the story of a grandmother and her granddaughter. Nothing more.

CHAPTER ONE

My earliest memory of my grandmother probably is sleeping spoon fashion with her in her bed. Snuggled up to her back with my big brother Charles, or "Bird" as he's known, behind me, the spoons were "rearranged" when we got fidgety or started kicking each other. Then she was the serving spoon and we were the two teaspoons on either side.

Me and 'Tine, as I called my grandmother, had spent so much time, most of my thirty-five years, saying what was on our minds—fighting, then making up on a daily basis. So I didn't have any *I'm sorry*s to say when she took to her death bed, just *thank-you*s. Instead, as she sat on the edge of the bed looking across the bay from her home on Dog Island, Florida, I asked her, "Do you know you are just about my favorite person in the whole world?"

She cocked her head and smiled. "No, no I didn't."

"Well, you are," I said nervously. "Do you know when I was little, I thought all grandmothers were just like you? I thought all grandmothers lived in the country in log cabins

1

and played games with their grandchildren and took them for walks . . ."

"Really?"

"All grandmothers should be like you," I said, calling forth the simple moments that had been imprinted on my brain. "And do you remember that game you taught me and how we made fairy rooms on the tree roots together? An acorn would be a cap, a leaf a bed, a stick a person, moss would be a carpet—do you remember that, 'Tine?"

"Did I do that?" she asked, full of innocence, pleased in spirit though her once-strong body slumped and her mind betrayed her.

"Yes. You did that. And remember at Round Lake drawing plans for the beach house in the sand? Adding the bedrooms and a long porch so that we could have bunk beds and everyone would have a place to sleep?"

"I did that too?"

"We used to dream about the beach house all the time— and you really built it."

"It's a good place, isn't it?" she asked, lying back against her pillows and closing her eyes to doze.

It wasn't adequate, I knew. I was trying to thank my grandmother for teaching me to "notice" the world—for every walk in the woods, for every smell, for every tiny detail that makes up life.

✇ I was born on June 19, 1964, at Crawford Long Memorial Hospital in downtown Atlanta. My father was in the Army and not attendant at my birth, so my mother named me Celestine Sibley Fleming for my grandmother. I like to hear my mother tell how she went into labor. Her sister and my grandmother were taking her to the hospital by way of slow and interested window-shopping. As her pains quickened and deepened, she was admonished to keep them to herself—who wanted to hang around hospital hallways waiting for a long labor?

When I came out into the world, I was covered in dark hair and my mother never tires of telling anyone who will listen that I looked just like a baby gorilla.

I doubt my appearance had anything to do with it, but my grandmother wasn't wild about me being saddled with her name. She'd never been overly enthusiastic about being named Celestine herself. When her mother, Evelyn Barber Sibley (known as Muv), was a young woman, Muv and a best friend had seen a boat called *The Celestine* and made a pact to each name their first born accordingly. Well, my great-grandmother had a little girl and named her Celestine. Course, it couldn't have been harder for her than it was for the baby boy who also was named Celestine. When the friend's child grew up—story has it—he had his name legally changed to something else.

So when my mother wanted to make me 'Tine's namesake, 'Tine said only on the condition that no one ever call me Celestine. Hence, I was named as many Southern women are, with a family surname for my first name—*Sibley*.

❦ I was pretty small when my grandmother sold her house in town and bought Sweet Apple, her 1840s cabin near Roswell, a suburb of Atlanta—so small that my first memories are of my grandmother already living there. Stories of earlier days might as well date back to the time of the dinosaurs—they just don't exist in my mind. In the beginning, my story goes, there was one log cabin and a goat shed at Sweet Apple. The goat's name was Winston so, of course, he was written into our family's version of the cigarette jingle:

Winston tastes good like a billy goat should,
No filter, no flavor, just like toilet paper!

✥ There was a stone well with a shingle roof that stood beside the cabin. My grandmother's biggest fear seemed to be that we little children would be drawn to it like a black hole. At the edge of the yard, on the side where it dips down into a gully, there was a swing. The seat was a fat flat board held up by thick twine ropes strung up high in an old oak tree, so high that the swing would glide far and long and slow.

I remember when I was small sitting at the top of the stairs in the cabin, thinking that 'Tine's house, with its living room, bedroom, kitchen, and porch, was the biggest, best place in the whole world. From under the floorboards came the sound of puppies squealing or grunting as they vied for position on the tits of their poor old mama dog. The smell in that house never did change—a bit of earth, pine, wax, dust, all mixed with a whiff of country air blowing freely between the unsealed logs. On the dining room table there was always a fresh arrangement of flowers—sometimes zinnias and bachelor's buttons from her garden, other times bowls of Queen Anne's lace or yellow forsythia branches from beside the road. In the winter, the standard arrangement was a bowl of small red apples stacked like a pyramid and accented by dark green sprigs of boxwood from around the front door.

A house with stairs. And under the sole set of stairs was a very dark bathroom with a curtained makeshift cupboard. Behind the curtain, my grandmother kept the family Christmas ornaments—an old angel from when her children were small; birds with glitter on their tails perched on golden nests filled with eggs; glass bulbs in blue and green and red; white wax candles with clips; and an assortment of homemade goodies like stale gingerbread men, desiccated popcorn strings, and faded paper chains with more glue than paper.

Back in those days, the late 1960s, 'Tine still had country neighbors whose country ways seemed to fit in with the season along with my great-grandmother Muv who came to visit from time to time. In the summer, there were building projects, a greenhouse, a treehouse, a seat around the apple tree. The vegetable garden, always ripe with the pungent smell of tomatoes and fresh-turned earth, was in constant need of weeding. There were stakes to hold up limbs and strings to direct wandering vines. In the last warm weeks of summer, there was the communal shelling of peas and beans in the yard. And, as cool weather set in, the gathering of three-foot-long oak logs for her fireplace, stacked thoughtfully in front of the silver gas tank.

I'm not sure why people dropped off their dogs by my grandmother's house, but they did. Just about any time you heard a car slowing down you could bet it was either a tourist or someone dropping off their mangy old dog. 'Tine always adopted them too. The standards in the pack became known as Stranger, Lightning, Lady, Manger, and Clyde—and those original dogs (and others) multiplied prolifically. So many puppies popped up in the spring that at one point there were easily a hundred. We kids loved it.

Every year there was a spring festival at Spring Street School, the elementary school my brother Bird and I attended in Atlanta. 'Tine and Jack, my grandmother's companion of nearly thirty years who officially became her second husband shortly before he died in 1985, thought up the dog-selling scam. The logic went that you couldn't give a dog away but if you put a small price on its furry little head, you could sell it. So they tied blue ribbons around the necks of, say, about fifty males and pink ribbons around the necks of the remaining fifty girls, loaded them in the back of their pick-up truck and took them to the school festival to sell for a dollar a piece. The puppies gave me some momentary rise in social status. What kind of luck did I have to possess a grandmother with so many adorable squealing mutts?

The spring festivals at Spring Street were family affairs. Everyone got involved. There was a dance around a maypole to the tune of a Mozart minuet, the children dressed in black patent leather shoes, lace, and clean white shirts. The pastel streamers from the pole were made of crepe, and wound around it innocently. At that same festival my mother dressed as a gypsy and told fortunes in one of the booths. I don't remember her fortunes but given her sense of humor, off-center as it is, I can only *imagine*. Her favorite joke, after all, was, "What is green, has four wheels, and a handle to pull it?" When we answered "A wagon! A wagon!", she would laugh with a certain coyness that I believe only young mothers can have and say, "Grass—and I lied about the wheels and the handle." An older parent might have told the joke with a more standard punch line that made life seem less absurd or more fair.

I got my fortune told and then went back to check on 'Tine and Jack, enjoying the disbelief on the faces of my fellow school chums that I indeed was connected with an enterprise that cool. Children who didn't have the dollar but wanted a puppy would receive a "loan" from Jack as long as they got their mothers' permission. When potential buyers—worried about their city houses, their city apartments, their city-sized yards—asked the probable size of the full-grown dogs, Jack would assure them with his Cajun Biloxi charm that indeed these puppies would grow to be quite small, convenient, smart, and affordable.

After getting a little spending money, I trotted around, ate a slab of fresh sugarcane, and then noticed the biscuit-eating contest, which I entered and lost as first runner-up, beaten by some boy twice my size. He got the prize and I got a stomachache.

My mother and her two siblings had gone to Spring Street School and I remember how proud Mom seemed to be that my brother and I were following in the family tradition. It must have been right after integration that we started school because I do not remember a time when things weren't racially mixed. My mother would wail out brightly on the way to school or on the way home, the school song:

> *Unfurl the colors purple and green, Spring Street School's*
> *the best ever seen!*
> *There I learned my ABCs! Reading and writing and one-*
> *two-threes!*
> *Though I know some day we'll have to part, Spring Street*
> *School will live in my heart.*
> *Classmates loyal, playmates too. So hail Spring Street*
> *School to you!*

Of course our favorite word was *hail* which we mistook for *hell*. *Hell* Spring Street School to you! After Mom sang the school's honor, she'd get this devious look on her face—a sort of mixture of false manners and evil—and she'd begin the next version:

> *Unfurl the colors purple and green, Spring Street School's*
> *the worst ever seen.*
> *Classmates loyal, werewolves too. So hell, Spring Street*
> *School to you!*

✀ I do not know what I thought about the *whys* or *where-fores* when 'Tine came to speak and sign books at Spring Street in those early years. I know simply that all the classes in the school would file into the auditorium as if for a play and she'd speak. I guess I didn't really think much about it at all—for all I knew, grandmothers held such a high place in society that it was good and right. I had a friend whose grandmother had written the first pressure cooker cook-book. There was another friend whose grandmother was a nurse. I know now that my grandmother came to speak at our schools because she was trying to help us out. Bird and I were garden-variety outcast-type kids, late for school most of the time, struggling to fit in with the system.

I was a strange child, quiet, shy, always to myself and out-side of the mainstream of chattering children. I was so self-conscious of the fact that I was taller by a head than the rest of the students that I would pretend I was invisible, not listen or ask questions, and daydream. So even when 'Tine was fin-ished with her speech and signing books and she'd come to my classroom with cookies for everyone and the children would gather round to show her stories they'd written, I still hung back. When she picked us up after school, I could only say, "Thanks for the cookies."

✀ One of the oddest things that we children accepted as fact were tourists. The word still makes me a little uneasy. Whenever we heard the crunch of tires on the dirt road in front of Sweet Apple, we paused like deers sensing a hunter— the smell of something foreign, perhaps dangerous in the air. We did not run unless we heard the danger creeping up my grandmother's long driveway, an entry hidden to all but the most persistent of sightseers. And that only meant one thing.

My grandmother would drop whatever was in her hands and call out, "Hide children! It's *tourists!*"

And so we played hide-and-go seek with her readers, her fans.

A favorite spot to hide in the summer was behind the garden—you could see *them* but they couldn't see *you*. Once when grandmother had sounded the alarm and we'd disposed of the sight of ourselves, we saw a woman and a man park in the driveway and get out of their car. They would not be so easily fooled by the strange silence (even the birds seemed to play along by stopping their song), and the woman kept shouting, "Anybody home? Hello! Anybody here?"

Feeling some guilt, I called out, "We're hiding in back of the garden!"

Of course, my grandmother then had to appear from her greenhouse where she'd been holding her breath, smooth out her apron, take up some clippers, and go be nice. That niceness meant offering a cold drink, sitting in the yard, listening, answering questions, and watching the day waste away, precious time going up in smoke. But that was the only time I ever invited tourists to find us. I learned what tourists could and would do to get what they wanted, including peering through windows and letting themselves in the back door.

✀ Me and my brother Bird spent a lot of time with 'Tine, maybe because we were the product of a teenage romance. Our parents were busy getting their lives off the ground and so, often enough, we stayed in the country with our grandmother who would fill in for our mother and pick us up after school. She arrived in a big lemon-yellow Cadillac wearing a wool skirt, cotton shirt, and loafers speckled with dirt. That was her work uniform. At home, she did good to match shoes, let alone socks. She wore whatever was comfortable and, because it was her, it was okay.

In the fall when the high winds blew, 'Tine and Jack would take me and Bird to her neighbors Doc and Verda's to fly kites in their pasture. We started with the cheap store-bought plastic kind and quickly graduated to making our own out of crepe paper and sticks. 'Tine encouraged us and bought us a book on how to make kites. We tried our hand at making Chinese box kites and other shapes. Sometimes they flew and sometimes they were just pretty to look at, like Easter parade floats. The best kites were the diamond-shaped ones with tails made from strips of white cotton bedsheets. Those were the ones that would catch the wind and stay up, tugging back at you like you were reeling in a big fish from the sky. And, as we flew our kites, we stepped in cowpatties—my mother assured us that only country children could appreciate the cool of manure squooshing between bare toes.

My mother passed on lots of old wives' tales and superstitions that she inherited from both my grandmother and great-grandmother. When the sun is shining and it's raining, you're supposed to put a stick in the ground and yell, "The devil's beating his wife!" A less enjoyable practice had to do with getting splinters. When Mom removed a splinter from one of us kids, she rubbed it into our hair for luck. On New Year's, family tradition held that whoever found a token of good fortune in their black-eyed peas would have luck the rest of the year. It seemed like some years Mom would add to the peas every piece from the Monopoly board, along with her wedding ring and a new dime. Everything is a sign with my mother, a feeling she inherited from Muv that my grandmother didn't get. My grandmother would talk about her old aunts reading coffee grounds. Although she'd refer to these and other customs, she wasn't a believer.

If my grandmother did believe in any signs at all, they were signs from God—not superstitions—and since she believed that one's relationship with God was highly personal, it wasn't something she'd share.

'Tine believed in hard work and secondly, *knowing*.

My grandmother taught us to identify the world around us and it was a gift that has lasted always. She believed that every child should recognize persimmon, black walnut, and pecan trees—as well as the fruit trees and the basic oaks and conifers. Likewise, every child should know a few roots—such as ginger and sassafras—from which to make tea. 'Tine's own repertoire extended to rocks and birds, mushrooms and seashells.

She was a natural natural*ist*. By her kitchen sink, she kept a compost bucket which got dumped and recycled into her garden. She grew marigolds to keep pests away instead of spraying insecticide. Although she may have let bread go moldy and milk go sour, she was careful not to let any large amount of food go to waste.

She was also a believer in gathering what food God saw fit to throw down for nothing. There were scuppernongs growing wild on the road to Jack's house and me and 'Tine and Bird would stop and pick them—sometimes they were sweet but most times they were not quite ripe and had a sharp sour flavor. In the summers, picking blackberries was a favorite freebie, as were the pecans that dropped in my great-grandmother Muv's yard. They aren't there anymore, but at one time 'Tine's sloping east yard was filled with cherry trees—a gift from Jack. The trees grew in a bending fashion like they were exercising and got stuck on their sides. For a kid, that meant an easy sitting place and a quick sweet snack. The apples from 'Tine's trees were mostly all green and sour and, while good for pies, are not what I'd call a pleasant casual food.

Towards nightfall, we'd sometimes use a trick we'd learned from one of the grownups—throwing rocks up in the air as we walked between the tall trees alongside the dirt road. The bats would think the rocks were food—bugs or whatever bats eat—and would try to catch them.

Me and Bird would tie strings around the back legs of June bugs to make little helicopters. When one of us caught a little box turtle, we'd paint our initials in frosty pink fingernail polish on its back, the impetus for us to let it go rather than set up a household for nature under our beds. 'Tine had told us if we put our initials on a turtle's back, the next time it was found, we'd know which one it was. (Painting turtles has since been proven an unsafe practice for them, but we didn't know that back then.)

My grandmother took up knitting because when she was growing up, country women crocheted and she, like the English, considered knitting to be more refined and ladified. She taught me to knit, a process that took much patience. I'd sit at 'Tine's feet on the footstool in front of the fireplace trying to remember which needle I was on last, getting her to fix a dropped stitch or assure me that holes gave my work "character."

When I got a little better, together we started an afghan made of pinwheels. The pattern was from a magazine. It was a project that promised to last many years—and did. She was taking knitting classes and had friends at the place in Roswell which sold wool. She also made sweaters for me—a less pleasing prospect. She'd get to a point close to finishing and discover I'd grown, so she'd take me in to measure and to get pointers on how to proceed with my new garment. The lady in the wool shop—mean, pinched-nosed, and with bad eyesight—would start off by looking at me and thinking I was a twelve-year-old boy instead of a nine-year-old girl. My hair was short and I was big. I *was* a tomboy and could hold my own most of the time with my brother and male cousins. My grandmother and my aunt would take me to either Rich's department store in downtown Atlanta for a "pixie" (a girl's crew cut) or to my grandmother's kitchen table for a bowl-and-rusty-scissor 'do. That was a time in my life I had already tired of saying what I tiredly told the wool lady, "*I'm a girl!*" Noting the truth, the woman proceeded to measure my shoulders, commenting on how she'd never seen such broad and wide shoulders on a little girl. I know my grandmother felt for me. On the one hand, she didn't encourage prissy behavior but, on the other, she understood what it felt like to be misclassified altogether. She'd talk about Jackie Kennedy—her shoe size, her height. She'd throw in something about Eleanor Roosevelt and other accomplished women who were big but who had style.

I liked our stuffed animal sewing projects and our doll dressmaking projects best, I think. Results could be achieved in an afternoon and you could immediately play with your efforts. We made dolls out of rolled-up dishclothes and painted their faces on with ink pens. She'd let me try my hand with the corn shucks when she was cooking supper, too. Corn shucks can be made into corn shuck dolls. The silk becomes hair. You fold the shucks just so and tie them off to make arms, head, and body. The bodies we made tended to be long skirts cut even at the hem.

Being the only girl among a brother and two male cousins, often enough I hung around the house, under 'Tine's heels.

When we were all about seven or eight years old (there were two consecutive batches of us—Bird and my cousin John were both born in 1963 and me and cousin Ted came along in 1964), 'Tine's country neighbors Larry and Quinton Johnson built a treehouse for the boys. For *my* playing pleasure, the women in our family—my aunt Susan, my mother, and 'Tine—cleaned out the old log corn crib and furnished it with honest-to-goodness pioneer-period furniture which was just right for a playhouse since women had been so much smaller a hundred or so years before.

The playhouse had a single window and was dark. It had a bed for my dolls and stuffed animals and a table for my pink rose tea set. Not being much of a housekeeper even then, I'd go in the playhouse, take a look around and either try to get the boys in trouble or hang out with 'Tine. Ted would play with me when the big boys wouldn't let him run with them. He said he was keeping up both sides, you know, just in case.

Jack's house was on a road which forked off of my grandmother's road and was probably built there just to keep my grandmother "respectable" when such things mattered. They weren't married then but they'd always lived together as far back as I could remember. When company that didn't know the arrangement came over, Jack could politely retire to his house.

Jack had some land and a lake where we children all learned to swim. We'd pile in the back of the truck and race the dogs from Sweet Apple cabin to the lake, we children standing dangerously behind the cab of the truck, the wind whipping our faces and the dips in the road lending excitement to our footing. Jack had built a cinder block wall in one corner of the lake to keep us safe while we were learning to float and both he and 'Tine repeatedly tried to install a white sand beach, but it sank promptly into the tall weeds and mixed with the murky bottom of the lake.

On the weekends and during summer, we'd wake up to find that 'Tine had been up for hours. Sometimes she'd have a desk set up on the back porch, other times it'd be under a window in her living room opposite the fireplace. "Let me get this column off" or "Let me get this chapter off and we'll take a walk, children," she'd begin cheerfully after her "Good morning." Her phone, a black wall number, was just inside the back door, so she could talk on the phone and observe her yard at the same time. On Sunday mornings, her regular call time, as often as not we'd get up to find her talking to Muv.

✂ And then there were birthdays. One of the best things about birthdays, in my estimation, was the birthday cake. I always had visions of cakes shaped like carousels with cookie cutter horses and colorful lace and ribbons made of icing. I would have been happy with a five-tiered wedding cake, perhaps in strawberry, or one of those cakes that ladies are reported to jump out of. *That big.*

My grandmother, however, did not believe in grocery store cakes. "We don't like those," I was told as I stood in front of the warm bakery window eyeing a bright cake with plastic toys stuck in the icing. (I used to think when I heard that ominous collective "we" that somehow I'd agreed to like or dislike something and had completely forgotten about it.) Well, *our* birthday cakes had to be homemade and that didn't include mixes or canned icing.

One of the more interesting cakes I recall was one my grandmother made from scratch. It had chocolate bits inside and, I remember, melted marshmallows on the outside. When she stuck the candles into it, they promptly fell like miniature trees in quicksand. "I made you a beautiful cake," she had explained—I think I was turning nine or ten that summer, "but as I was walking it down the road, a mama bear jumped out from behind the bushes. She told me it was her little bear's birthday today and if I didn't trade cakes with her, she'd eat me up. So while the cake I actually made was gorgeous, the one we have is unfortunately the one that that poor desperate mother bear made."

In that particular instance, the story was better than the cake. No matter how old I got, I just wanted to believe those stories, to think that there were talking bears in the woods. I was slow to even want to mature. Every time my mother wanted to get rid of one of my dogs, she'd say it went to some poor crippled child who was an orphan, who lived in the country alone—until he got my dog. I wanted to believe that. It sounded so much better than the truth, that the dog probably went to the Humane Society or to the pound.

We stayed with 'Tine off and on, sometimes with our aunt and uncle and cousins. My uncle would get me up in the morning saying, "There's a lady at the door giving away ponies," and without fail, every morning, I'd jump up and run to the door to see. "You just missed her," he'd say. I'd have to be quicker the next time.

✎ The best place me and my brother and parents ever lived was across the Little River from 'Tine in the old Dean Rusk homestead in Cherokee County. (Rusk had served as President Kennedy's secretary of state.) There were many other places I called home before and after our two years in the country but none captured my domestic affections, or my heart, so well.

It was back in the early seventies. There was a blackberry patch at the bottom of the field just at the edge the wood. At the far end of the pasture was a pig named Roscoe, a path to a little river, an old cemetery filled with folks from the Indian days, and a wild persimmon tree.

We had animals in abundance. My brother built wagons for the two donkeys, Jenny and Jack, that 'Tine and Jack bought us and our cousins. Though decidedly lazy, Jenny and Jack were sometimes good for a downhill race through the pasture to the river.

The donkeys were not alone in the pasture, however. Our neighbors kept an old mule called Tom, a gentle quarter horse named Sunday, and two spirited horses of breeding that were not broken in and tended to kick when one forgot to walk the right way around them.

A patchwork garden by our mother's kitchen was filled with odds and ends of produce—miniature watermelons here, red tomatoes there, a row of lettuce mixed with a variety of weeds like ready-made salad.

The house itself was as old as the cemetery. Its weathered boards, which once might have been painted, were washed down to their natural gray and the tin on the roof had rusted orange.

A wraparound porch neatly skirted the house on all but one side. From the front porch you could see a dirt road which picked up where the orange daylilies left off. In the fall, spring, and summer, the porch also functioned as a dining room. A side porch faced south towards the pasture, a good place to hide from chores in the heat of the day and for watching sunsets in the cool of the evening.

On the back porch off the kitchen was an old washing machine with a roller to wring out wet clothes. Of course there were more modern styles of washing machines available then but it was a time when the world had suddenly rediscovered the basics. It was the hippie era when people our parents' age were going "back to nature."

The back porch faced an outdoor shower, an outhouse, and, further down, a barn where animals—billy goats, wild chickens, and spiders—gathered on two legs, four legs, and more.

Sometimes, the animals were of the human variety, friends of our parents on a journey to find themselves in spite of the fact any mirror would have told them they were camped out in the top of a barn infringing on our play space.

One of our favorite play goals as children was to get our grandmother to participate in games. On long summer days out in the country we tried to teach her the rules of Parcheesi, Monopoly, and Go Fish, to no avail. Games, whether on a board or dealt out of a deck, we told her, eased boredom.

"Boredom?" she whispered, as if we'd introduced a new species of animal into the ecosystem. "That worries me, children," she would shake her head. To our grandmother, the mere possibility that anyone could get bored was a sinister indication of a bleak future.

She herself had never experienced the vaguest feeling of restlessness. There were never enough hours in any given day for our grandmother to accomplish what she wanted, let alone time for mindless activity.

Instead of sluggishly rising late in the morning, she bounded out of bed at 3:00 A.M. to greet the day, excited about the possibilities—known and unknown. By the time we children woke up, our grandmother would have already weeded a flowerbed, cooked breakfast, said her prayers, and fed and watered her animals. As we ate, she expounded gloriously upon the qualities of oatmeal and its effects upon children's constitutions. Having cleaned our cereal bowls, we then accompanied her on her daily walk down the dirt road that ran beside her cabin.

Since I've been grown, I like to think that perhaps some of my grandmother's philosophy took hold. I do not race the sun as a matter of course, nor have I ever acquired the knack of warming up a room with sweet smells or the cheerful sound of my voice. But a common trait, I suppose, is a shared and heretofore unexpressed belief that every moment is precious, that it is not enough to eat and breath and sleep and stay out of jail. And we shared the belief that the antidote to mindless games is, of course, books.

When we were growing up we not only had books, we had *all* books. We were never denied any reading that we wanted. The many hours a week I borrowed from sleep time for my reading got so out of control at one point that an inner struggle ensued as to how I could validate so much reading purely for pleasure. I had thought about eliminating the habit altogether and was telling that same gameless grandmother just that when she offered me a book on Josephine and Napoleon. It was good, she told me. She couldn't put it down.

"Then I won't borrow it," I said with great willpower.

"I know what you mean," she said, herself prey to the same habit. "You don't have to quit, just curb."

❦ Once a business acquaintance told me how lucky I was, being my grandmother's granddaughter, how if she were me, she'd take advantage of all of *my* connections. What an interesting notion, I thought at the time, the things people come up with. But then, maybe things look different from the outside than they are in reality.

Here's reality. When my brother and I were eleven and twelve years old respectively, we paged at the Georgia state legislature for Grace Towns Hamilton, the first black woman member of the House of Representatives. It was twenty dollars to us for a week's worth of work and five days off from school. "Don't expect any special favors," my teacher had told me pointedly in front of the class at the beginning of the school year, so she was less than receptive to the idea of me getting the special privilege of paging. I wasn't sure what she had been talking about, but it left me with a vague feeling that something was different about me.

As for paging, we had already spent plenty of time playing in the state capitol after school and we hung out in the press box when the House was in session waiting for 'Tine to finish up work. We explored the natural history exhibits on the second floor, looked the gargantuan statues of statesmen, and slid down the marble stair rails.

Back in the late seventies, paging wasn't as organized as it is now. Today, all the well-dressed clean children are lined up on a bench in the hall outside the chamber, waiting patiently until they're called to duty. They are overseen by adults.

But not in my day. We were trained enough to know that pages were supposed to get refreshments for their bosses and retrieve copies of bills and other paperwork. But I don't recall ever doing anything useful for Ms. Hamilton. I spent a lot of time in the side room gallery drinking free chocolate milk, sitting in empty representative's chairs watching the speaker, or scouting out the room from up in the balcony until the day was done.

One afternoon, after a particularly grueling day of clothes shopping (we always hit the thrift stores first, trying on piles of unfashionable clothes in cramped rooms with bad lighting) me and my grandmother ended with lunch at Rich's department store, then headed back to the capitol. In the hall, we met then-governor George Busbee. My grandmother introduced us.

The governor told us to come with him to his office and he'd have the capitol photographer take my picture with him.

"Nonsense," my grandmother told him, "you're too busy running the state for such foolishness." I was deflated.

Still, Governor Busbee sent his photographer and let me get my picture made sitting behind his desk. It has always been a thorn in my side when I look at that photograph and think of what could have been. I explain it away, thinking, "The governor wanted to have his picture made with me, but 'Tine wouldn't let him."

A couple of Christmases, we got to go pick out anything we wanted from Rich's—thanks to Faith Brunson, my grandmother's close friend and a legendary book buyer for the store. Faith took us to ride the Pink Pig, a Christmas tradition—nay, an *institution* in Atlanta. The Pink Pig, which resembled a small-town carnival ride in the shape of a smiling pink pig, was set up on the roof of the downtown Rich's each holiday season. The miniature track wound its way through a small forest of Christmas trees and lights. After the ride, Faith would say "whatever you want." Of course, we wouldn't have picked out a living room set or a gas range, but even a sleeping bag was a big deal back then.

There were other perks too, like freebies from the *Atlanta Journal-Constitution*—books and tickets. Since my grandmother kept a Christmas bag in her office for things she received, we got a lot of interesting items that most people might never have thought about buying—little bags of real cotton from the Georgia Department of Agriculture, fireproof clothing in which we dressed up as space creatures.

When December rolled around, 'Tine, who basically hated to shop and hated materialism in just about any form, would start wrapping stuff that public relations people had sent her throughout the year. That's why we got in the habit of shaking the books we received from her on Christmas morning, shaking them to get rid of the press releases the publishers always stuck inside them.

✻ Bird and I didn't receive a royalty, but we liked to think we helped her write her books. One particular book that my brother and I worked very hard on was her 1975 collection of quotations, *Day by Day with Celestine Sibley.* We'd get up and ride with 'Tine to town, park and head towards the old library. But first we'd have to stop at Dunkin' Donuts for as many donuts as we could stomach. *Then* it was off to the library. My grandmother working the stacks, taking notes, and me and Bird (who's actually a speed reader and has been since he was two) would spend the day exploring the library just as we'd explored the state capitol.

From time to time, we'd hear that one of her writer friends—mystery author Wylly Folk St. John, for one—was using us as characters for a new book. There were people around who were probably famous, but my favorite that I remember—though I didn't know of his fame at the time— was Joe David Brown, author of *Addie Pray*, the book on which the 1973 movie *Paper Moon* was based. He'd come to the country with his wife Fran in their Jeep with a cooler full of black salamanders to be used as bait. There'd be some sort of cookout and fishing at Jack's lake.

But what really made the Browns so special in my young mind was the fact that Joe David let me sit in his lap and drive his Jeep off the road and into a deep ditch one evening. So what can you say? I didn't get anything about *fame* or *celebrity* or any of that when I was a kid. I'm not sure I've digested it completely as an adult. Nor have my sons, Vincent and Wolfie. When 'Tine died, Wolfie, seeing his great-grand-mother all over TV, asked, "Was 'Tine *famous?*"

CHAPTER TWO

The night before my grandmother would make her last trip to East Bay in Holley, Florida, where she was born, and to Muv's house in Alford, Florida, she called me.

"You're going to be the family historian," she said, "you should be coming on this trip." She was planning on visiting the grave of her biological grandfather, Henry Colley Senior, and the little church where Muv had fended off raucous well-wishers on her wedding night with a hat pin. I knew where Muv's grave was in Alford—I grew up with my mother taking us over to the town's modest cemetery and pouring a "cold one" onto the hard ground the way some people bring flowers. (Of this quaint tradition, my grandmother was unaware.)

And that is something I will always regret, that I didn't take time off from what I thought was pressing and necessary, to see and listen. When my great-grandmother Muv was a couple of weeks from death, she had tried to get my grandmother to listen to her, to tell her stories about the ones who had come before, who they were, where they were buried. But my grandmother wouldn't listen. Instead she cleaned out cupboards stocked with forty years of saved glass jars and bleach bottles. She cleaned under cabinets, threw things out, dusted and scrubbed, keeping herself too usefully busy to sit. Then Muv died and she took her stories with her. Twenty-odd years later, history repeated itself.

In September of 1997, my grandmother and I went to a book convention in Mobile, Alabama. We'd stopped by Peachtree Publishers on the way out of Atlanta to look at fresh-shipped copies of *The Celestine Sibley Sampler*. She hadn't seen it the whole time I was putting it together. She trusted me, or if she didn't exactly trust me, she knew I'd have to live with her when it was done.

It is a small press so everyone who worked at Peachtree came and gathered around my grandmother and me. It wasn't just my editorial project or her writing, it was a labor shared by many people, from production to sales. We all piled up in the conference room around a long meeting table, stacks of books were brought in like baskets of bananas, the festivity welled up, and the room was filled with the hopeful expectancy of my grandmother's approval. She looked at the new book as all authors do, like a parent examining a new baby, checking to see that it has all of its fingers and toes. It is one of the unique things about books that, like children, no matter how many you have, each one comes out as a sort of miracle.

We all sighed a long wind of relief as she began to *ooh* and *aah*, leafing through the raw-cut pages, marveling at photographs we'd managed to pull together, at the kind words her friends had written about her. I knew she was pleased with the outcome when she began to sign copies for the staff. When someone brought the book over for me to sign too,

'Tine asked, half-serious, half-joking, "She doesn't get to sign my book, does she?"

That was the seal of approval. It was then *her* book and to hear her claim ownership made all the hard work worth while. A couple of boxes were loaded into the trunk of my car and off we went down the highway, gossiping with great expectation for our long weekend. Not only were we going to a book convention (which meant free books and time to talk shop with old friends) but we were going to see family things around Mobile as well.

Since 'Tine had spent many of her early years in nearby Creola, Alabama, there would be plenty of family to visit, as well as graveyards and old homes. There too was my maternal grandfather's side of the family, an old and distinguished people who sprang up in my mind like characters in a distant fairy tale.

We went to the Methodist cemetery in Creola first. "I want to see everyone," I said, opening the door of the car which was parked in a swarm of black lovebugs.

I knew the Hatter's plot from previous visits and went straight to the iron gate that had been painted white over a century and a half of rust. After I said hello to Pap (Wesley Reeder Sibley), to Muh' Dear (Ophelia Hatter Sibley), and the rest, I begged to see Hatter's Mill, where my grandmother grew up after Muv married Pap, a lumberman, in 1924. The mill pond was supposed to still be there. But my grandmother was the kind of reluctant which resembles the effect you get when you hold a magnet up to a compass. Her sense of direction failed, I think out of fear of what she'd see. Memories of a happy childhood were too delicate to defile with change.

On the deep sand road by the cemetery, I spotted an old gentleman in overalls walking unevenly, the shifting earth throwing him off balance. He held an umbrella over his head, a shield against the sun. I peeled up slowly alongside him—against my grandmother's protestations—and asked about the mill.

"We'll never find it now," 'Tine complained after we thanked the man for the directions he'd given.

"Yes, we will. That gentleman knew where the pond was. It hasn't been forgotten," I insisted.

It was easier for me because I did not remember the way things *were*. I closed my eyes and savored the stories.

"See this bridge? Pap was coming down this road—it was just dirt then—in a flat wagon. He met a bear on the bridge. Pap wasn't hurt, but ever after he kept looking for that bear . . .

"There were alligators in the mill pond and Pap had decided to catch them using my puppies Hans and Fritz as bait. I cried and cried but he said he'd be standing there with his shotgun and get the alligators before the gators got the puppies. He tied them to a log but they never did make any noise and attract the alligators. Hans and Fritz just fell asleep."

Of all the eccentric family stories I've heard over the years, none has been more intriguing than that of my great-great-grandmother, Sue Hinson Barber, who was what was called "a traveling woman." She was Muv's mother, 'Tine's grandmother.

Sue, as I understand it, was beautiful among her plain sisters and had an air of mischief. Her parents, simple country folk, married her off when she was sixteen years old to a well-to-do forty-year-old farmer by the name of John Barber. After their first child was born, Sue slipped out the back door with the baby and started a life of wandering.

The poor distraught husband, John Barber, went after his young wife unsuccessfully and eventually his mind slipped away—it has been said that he was committed down at the

Georgia State Sanitarium in Milledgeville where he died and was buried. I asked 'Tine repeatedly to share the details of John Barber's sad life but always drew blanks. There were so many other more respectable genes inscribed in our bones and weedy graves, memories of forefathers to gather from the dust of old pieces of broken furniture and leftover silver odds and ends, why did I have to pick the worst of the worst to glorify?

Well, it wasn't my intention to *glorify*, exactly. I just wanted to know what all was floating around in the gene pool. I wanted to know how much of our little family culture was set by nature, how much had been handed down like a cake recipe without baking soda.

Not to be deterred, I began my research at Milledgeville. If everyone can trace themselves back to Queen Victoria and Charlemagne, I figured you could also trace lineage back to Ivan the Terrible and Judas.

The archivist was a kindly man who sounded a bit embarrassed that a granddaughter—even a great-great one—would want to know about her crazy kin. Though I obviously couldn't see his face over the telephone, I could hear in his tone that his office wasn't the usual pit stop of family genealogists. Seeing that I was indeed serious about my search, the archivist took my phone number and within an hour called me back. Yes, there had been a John Barber at Milledgeville who had died in the institution and had been buried there in 1906.

"An unmarked grave?" I asked.

"Our graves are *not* unmarked. They have little steel posts with numbers and we can tell you where your great-great-grandfather is buried if you'd like to come see."

I thanked the archivist and said if I came down to look for the grave, I'd certainly pay him a visit. Then, closing my eyes, I imagined Sue, her long red hair flowing in the breeze as she paced back and forth, calling for her daughter, Dixie, who I knew as Muv, to come.

I made a mental picture of the child Dixie who had just gotten "situated" again, who hid from her mother while the leaving filled the air. And as I opened my eyes, there was just a film of an image: Sue's feet shuffling through the dirt, making wreaths of dust on the open road as she walked away—and left her daughter.

My great-grandmother Muv was married twice and at the same time. After a childhood of being "poor kin," she married Henry Colley, whose father ran a general store and post office in East Bay. My grandmother was born Celestine Broxson Colley. A second child, a boy, came a few years later and was named Vernon Castle for the famous dancer. Henry Colley Senior died not long after 'Tine was born and, because of her father's lack of interest in work, the store was soon lost, as was the house which Henry Senior had built on the Yellow River in 1871 for his bride Susan Broxson.

In her 1988 memoir, *Turned Funny,* my grandmother explained that when the house and the store were gone, the Colleys moved to Bagdad, a little mill town to the north, and Little Henry went out looking for work. But having found employment, Little Henry refused to actually work—he wasn't bad-natured, just not endowed with much get-up-and-go.

Soon the local store refused my great-grandmother credit because Henry wasn't good for the bill. Once, after her credit had been cut off, she'd gone into the store to get some food for her children and the baby Vernon Castle reached out for a red apple saying, "Ap! Ap!" Because of her pride, my great-grandmother slapped his little hand away. My grandmother had always told me how guilty Muv had felt—the guilt never leaving her—that her baby was starving and she'd slapped his hand.

Not long after the incident with the apple, Vernon Castle got sick and listless. A black sharecropper family took them in and tried to feed him chicken gruel but he still died. My grandmother told me she remembered how nice they'd been to her, this family, even making her a doll out of a dishrag.

I was talking to my cousin John Bazemore, the oldest of my generation, about our family's fate. On August 14, 1999, the day before my grandmother died, his baby son had been taken to the emergency room. The baby displayed the same symptoms as the baby Vernon Castle. John told me it looked as if his child's condition was genetic, an inherited condition.

"I find it ironic," John told me, "that all those years 'Tine probably felt guilty because her little brother starved and she lived—but Vernon probably didn't starve at all, and we didn't figure that out until a week after she died."

It was plain in his voice, this oldest of grandchildren, that John would have liked to have lifted this burden.

One weekend when I was out in the country, scanning over the bookshelves at Sweet Apple, my grandmother gave me a book about Queen Victoria that had been hers as a child. The inscription in the front, written in childish hand, was "Celestine Broxson." I asked my grandmother about it, telling her I always thought her name was Colley before she'd been adopted by Pap and had become a Sibley.

"My middle name was Broxson," she told me in the dim light of her living room. "That was when Muv was hiding me from my father—she wouldn't let me use *Colley*," she clarified.

Having also been torn from family through my parents' divorce, I think I shared with my grandmother the grief that is associated with impossible childhoods.

Growing up, I had always been curious about my parents' first child, Richard, who had died when he was a baby, before my brother and I were born. It was silly, but I always imagined if he had lived, he could have given me piggyback rides—I thought of him as bigger though he had died so young. My mother never wanted to talk about Richard—I guess no one ever gets over the loss of a baby.

In any case, I think Little Henry tried to see my grandmother for a while after Muv left him, even tried to get his child to stay with him permanently but Muv was having none of that. Muv'd married Wesley Reeder Sibley, known in our family as Bob or Pap, telling him that my grandmother was in fact her niece. When my grandmother would slip and begin to say *Mama*, she'd catch herself and the abbreviated slip became *Muv*.

I asked my grandmother if she'd ever tried to see her father or to find him later. She told me sadly that once he'd gotten in touch with her after he read about her in the newspaper and she'd assumed he wanted money, that he thought maybe she'd done well. Her words were bitter because I don't think she ever stopped being angry at the parent who, at least in *her* mind, had abandoned her. But worse than bitterness, there was regret—he was one of the few people that she couldn't bring herself to forgive no matter how hard she tried. She blamed him for the death of her brother, for the part of her childhood when Muv had had to struggle to keep them going.

The struggle was so hard that one day she'd given up and left my grandmother at an orphanage until she could find some way to take care of her properly. Walking down the path away from the orphanage and her only child, Muv had second thoughts and turned right around before she hit the street, marched back up the path and retrieved her child. As my grandmother told me proudly, Muv said the conditions were so bad that she "wouldn't have left a dog in that place."

"When my biological father contacted me," my grandmother told me. "I asked him if he needed anything. He said, 'What help could you possibly be to me now?'"

That was a twist, I'm sure, because he could have been so much help to Muv—and wasn't. 'Tine told me her father had gone blind and there were strings running from room to room in his house to help him navigate. A neighbor lady—maybe it was a social worker—brought his meals every day and left them on a windowsill.

'Tine had never known, or not that she told me, when Henry Colley had died, where he was buried, or any of the things that bring comfort and finality. She had never had what today we call *closure*, a term foreign to her vocabulary.

My grandmother had come to feel that Pap, the one who had cared for her, sacrificed as loving parents do, watched her grow, and given her opportunities, was her real father. Since Pap died so long before I was born, I only know him from stories and photographs but hold him in high esteem. There are pictures in our old family photo albums, pictures from the twenties in which he looks so handsome and so pleased to have my great-grandmother beside him. One of the favorite stories my grandmother told me was how when she and Muv came to live with him, Pap had bought her a little hound dog named Welcome to welcome her to her new home.

When I was gathering 'Tine's papers to send to the archives at the Robert W. Woodruff Library at Emory University, I unearthed a poem called "Little Brown Coat" she'd written when she was around seven or eight years old. I fell so in love with her childish and candid feelings that I asked her for the poem to keep. With as little regard for her early words as for a finger painting, she gave the poem to me, wondering that I would want such a crude thing. It reads:

Dear Mr. Sibley I'm writing this note
asking you to please buy me a coat.
Now the coat which I have in view
comes in ether brown or blue
and the price is only 2.98
and if you don't hurry it will be to late
another little girl will buy it and leave
and I will have to wear my old one on Christmas eve.
I can do without a dress and a new hat to.
But I do want that brown coat and so would you.
The coat I am wearing is faded and green
and when I put it on I'm shame to be seen.
When I was younger I wanted a white goat
some children would want a balloon to float
and maybe you want a motor boat
but I would be the happest girl in town
if I had only that little coat of brown.

When she wrote about the poem in her book *Turned Funny,* it was as a thank-you note rather than a please-may-I-have?

Another childhood item I found that I asked for was a certificate from Pap marked "Merchants Bank, Mobile, Ala., Dec 19, 1924, No. 1." It reads: "Pay to the order of That Little Little old ugly Freckled Face Gal, $1 Switch, 1 Extra Heavy Switch," and then it's signed by "Her Old Buddy."

✂ Muv was always making clothes. There's a picture of my grandmother when she was hardly more than eight years old. She's in a bathing suit and posed as if she were jumping off a diving board. I showed it to her and she laughed.

"Muv was always making clothes for me and sending pictures to her relatives, trying to make me look good," she mused.

Then, she pointed out the chickens at the edge of the photograph. "That wasn't a pond I was jumping into—it was the chicken coop. Muv just made a prop out of a plank to make it look like I was diving into water . . ."

Not only that, but I think that Muv would rosy up my grandmother's cheeks with a little rouge and she wasn't beyond primping and curling her little daughter.

A friend of my great-grandmother's had commented on my grandmother when 'Tine was small, "She's not very P-R-E-T-T-Y, is she?", to which my grandmother replied, "No, but I'm S-M-A-R-T."

My grandmother never did think she was pretty, in spite of the fact that she was tall, thin, and very striking. She attributed her lumbering size and spacious feet to her biological father who was over six feet tall. It was true that my grandmother wasn't one of those run-of-the-mill blonde beauties and she confirmed that all of her life, reminding us all that she thought of herself as plain. When my grandmother was young, my mother remembers 'Tine as being beautiful and would never let anyone say otherwise. Even as 'Tine aged and her face was covered in wrinkles and lines, she was beautiful. There was something inviting in it, some kind of warmth to the way it was all put together.

When Pap was dying, Muv, oddly enough, was still legally married to Henry Colley. My grandmother was already grown and married and the mother of three children. Muv's lawyers advised her to quickly get a divorce and straighten out the first marriage if she wanted to keep her claim to Pap's estate. And, I think at Pap's insistence, she went through the motions. In the end, when legal minds said she could keep her claim as a common-law wife, she walked away saying that her husband's relatives could have all the money, an amount which would still be considered a small fortune. "It never made them happy anyway," she is reported to have said. Muv stayed in Alford until she died.

 ℋ I never knew Pap and Muv died when I was nine years old. My childhood memories were of her as an old lady with long gray hair tucked up in a roll on the back of her head, of Clorox jugs with the top halves cut off to receive her snuff spit, of a little black poodle she doted on named Jackie. Her neighbors called her Miss Sibley with respect and I think that that respect was important to her. She'd treated us, me and my brother Bird, two of her four great-grandchildren, sweetly. In the summer, we might go visit her in Alford for a week or two. She'd rouse us early from bed. The tiny kitchen was already heated up with pancake making. She let us drink children's coffee, three parts milk and sugar and one part coffee.

 Under a window that let in a flood of bright morning light, there was a rickety two-seater table which left just enough room to get by if one walked sideways. There, me and my brother sat and ate until we were stuffed. She wouldn't stop cooking while we could still fit a bite of food into our mouths.

 Through that little kitchen window, you could see her back steps to the right and her screened porch to the left. The yard was partitioned off by hedges and borders as if into little rooms. It seems as if there were dozens of sheds but more likely there were only a couple. We were relegated to her sun porch for our crafts, things that had to do with glitter, glue, and crayons. The windows went all the way around the walls and let the sun feed her collection of African violets. I have two constant memories of Muv: the first is of her sitting in a yard, her own or my grandmother's, with a bowl in her lap and a paper bag by her side, shelling peas (it seemed like she was always preparing vegetables); and the second is just a ghost of a vision of her passing through her house, a silhouette.

"I wish you could have known her when she was young," my grandmother always said wistfully. She wanted me to know the person she had known; I imagine the same way I one day will want my grandchildren to remember 'Tine. She never tired of telling me stories, of pointing out things that "Muv would like."

❧ In our family, at least I know it was true with my grandmother as it is for me, house improvements come with guests. Whenever I had a party or company that required getting ready for, my grandmother bequeathed me family items. I treasure the glass party plates with a beaded ruffle at their edges which Muv bought at dime stores. Muv liked pretty things that made up home and the plates had been bought for her own parties. They have no monetary value but every time I look at them, they remind me of Muv.

When 'Tine lent them to me, the plates were wrapped carefully in newspaper and as I lifted them out of my grandmother's car trunk, I was told, "I'm not giving them to you yet—they were Muv's."

"Muv was having some ladies over from the church when she bought these," my grandmother mused, unwrapping the dishes on my kitchen counter. "She wanted to invite a whore lady and she got some trouble from her nice friends . . ."

Apparently, my great-grandmother defended her choice in company and told the naysayers that it was her party and she'd invite whomever she chose. I liked that about her, that she wouldn't cast people off just because of what others thought. It was not an easy gesture to make in a small town and, to me, it showed real backbone. Funny that such ladified plates could hold such meaning.

Four months after she was diagnosed with terminal cancer, I was the fortunate recipient of a couple of my grandmother's prized possessions, namely, her dining room table and her bed. The table 'Tine fed her children on—I thought perhaps my mother would want it. But when I called and asked her, Mom was firm.

"'Tine wants you to have it," she said. Knowing the sentimental value it must hold for her, I said fine, but if she ever changed her mind, I'd load it up and bring it over.

My grandmother was more direct when I backed off from the heirloom. "You don't like it?" she asked, taking offense.

"No, 'Tine, I like it fine," I said. "I just don't know what you would do without it. What will you feed people on?"

"The table on the porch which used to be the dining room table," she indicated the long dark plank table on which her summer meals were often served by candlelight. "Just as soon as I can get one of the boys to fix the top, take off the boards with the burn holes . . ."

Obviously, she had a project in mind. With my particular grandmother once she had taken to an idea, stopping her was about as foolish as asking the wind not to blow.

She called around and found a lumberyard which we drove to over railroad tracks, by shanty shotgun houses, and around old brick factories. She had the measurements for the planks she needed and the boards were cut and loaded into the trunk of her car. Her project was going off that weekend. If she couldn't get one of the boys, she reasoned, it shouldn't be that hard to replace a tabletop herself.

I told my husband Ron about 'Tine's plans and he got up early Saturday morning and drove to the country without question. If no one showed up, he'd be ready to fill in the gap.

Well, my mother's husband, Ron Vance, was already at Sweet Apple. After I don't know how many phone calls and the end of the day, the table was finished, stained, and moved into the living room of 'Tine's little log cabin.

"So next time Ron comes," she said, out of breath from directing the work crews, "he can get *your* dining room table out of the annex."

Life with 'Tine would have been easier, I'm certain, if I could have just told my grandmother what to do, but the problem was, she didn't listen. She did what she wanted. And that's how it came to be that the next weekend we drove the truck back out to the country and got her bed.

Beds, like dining room tables, were a thing with my grand-mother. She didn't believe in sleeping on futons as Ron and I had been doing since we moved into our new house. She believed that futons were dog beds. Real beds had fresh clean sheets, dust ruffles, and bedposts to hang your robe on.

"'Tine," I said with trepidation, "we're not taking your bed."

"I may move into the downstairs bedroom," she waved me off, "for a change of scenery."

Now as long as I'd been alive, I'd known her views on the downstairs bedroom which was strictly reserved for company. The room is dark. It's big stone fireplace lets in a funnel of the kind of cold that most people only feel when they are outside.

"We're not taking your bed," I said as seriously as the ignored can be.

As proof of my earnestness, we went out to the old goat shed which was jam-packed with old furniture, beds, broken lawn mowers. That is where our bed would come from, I said, if we could not sleep on a futon. Unfortunately, there wasn't a complete bed, just odd slats and headboards. Leaving the bed situation behind, I went to the store for lunch.

When I got back, the truck was loaded with my grand-mother's dining room table and her bed. I went upstairs to inspect the emptiness of her bedroom. Plumb in the center, she'd moved the single bed. She was triumphant. "Franklin and Eleanor Roosevelt both slept in single beds," she said.

One thing 'Tine had omitted when she was making her plans is that although she could fit nicely into a single bed, her books, magazines, newspapers, and tissues could not be squeezed in there with her.

In May of 1993, 'Tine was awarded an honorary doctorate in the humanities from Spring Hill College, a Jesuit institution in Mobile, Alabama. 'Tine had attended the college from 1933 to 1936, while also working full-time at the *Mobile Press-Register*. I drove down to Spring Hill alone in my Volkswagen Beetle. It was my job to pick up her old friend, Ann Battle Hawkins, the former society editor at the *Press-Register*. As we drove to the commencement ceremonies, Ann delighted in telling me stories about my grandmother which, I imagine, have become standards in her repertoire.

"When the first helicopter—it was called a gyro-copter or something like that—came to Mobile," Ann began, "the editor wanted me to go up in it and write about it but I told him my mother wouldn't let me, so your grandmother went instead. She would get into anything that would lift off the ground."

I could imagine my grandmother, a teenager, thrilled at the prospect. She relished the unknown. In fact, only a couple of months before she died, she was riding on the back of a Harley Davidson with her friend Akili Ramsess from work—her first time on a motorcycle.

After my grandmother had been fully doctorized at Spring Hill, Ann took her aside. I had apparently made an impression.

"Sibley needs to make her bows to Mobile society," Ann said solemnly. Of course she was thinking of my grandfather and his cousins, distant to me, those genteel relatives who still held the reins of the city's society.

My grandmother scoffed, "Ann, Sibley is twenty-eight years old, divorced, and has two children. She's hardly *presentable.*"

Not that I appreciated such a description. Why couldn't I take up the family line, don some long white gloves and, you know, *bow*?

Ann would not be put off so easily. "Then we'll have a tea for her, as used to be done at the Battle House," she insisted, referring to Mobile's once-glorious 1908 hotel.

My grandmother let it go.

I am romantic about such things as society, in spite of what may have happened between my grandparents. I didn't build up the grandfather I never knew to be a demon drunkard womanizer—the charming, funny, eccentric stories about James William Little III were the ones that stuck in my mind. I did not grow up knowing my grandfather's family, just hearing and knowing the names that perpetuated their existence with each passing generation.

In his younger days, my grandfather was what was called a "deb's delight." And apparently there had been some debutante waiting in the wings who was considered the perfect match for him. As it was told to me, my great-grandfather had been very well off and invested heavily in the Florida building boom of the 1920s. When the boom went bust, he lost everything except for the house in Mobile. Not long after, he died of a heart attack and the family woke up to find they were penniless. The way my grandmother used to tell it, they were all very stoic and fell to, doing whatever they could to make ends meet. My great-grandmother Mamie took in boarders, my aunt Everitt went to work, as did my grandfather Jim, who got on with the *Press-Register* as a copyeditor.

Already, my grandmother was hot stuff in her field—she certainly wasn't debutante material but it was clear she was a young woman with drive and a bright future. It wasn't surprising that my grandfather was interested.

She told me he'd proposed when they'd gone for a walk in the woods together. He'd made a ring for her out of clover flowers and slipped it on her finger. She hadn't exactly wanted to marry him so much as she hadn't wanted to hurt his feelings, she told me. So she married him.

But we grandchildren didn't get to hear much about our grandfather when we were growing up. My mother said he used to playfully "beat the drums" on her back as a child and the way she talked about him, flirtatiously, as the youngest often are, one could tell that if she wasn't the fond favorite with him then he sure was with her.

He was the creator of our family tooth fairy, White Rat the Paper Hanger, who has endured now for more than half a century. White Rat was a gangster's name and, of course, a "paper hanger" was the colloquial term for a counterfeiter once upon a time. When my mother was small and later when me and Bird were losing our baby teeth, I'm pretty sure White Rat bought our teeth with counterfeit dollars.

When my little brothers, David and John-Stephen, came along many years later, Mom told them that White Rat got his money knocking over liquor stores. I decided to tell my sons, Vincent and Wolfie, that White Rat hung out beneath the sidewalk grates collecting the lost quarters which fell out of the pockets and purses of passersby. And that somehow, somehow, when White Rat had five dollars, somewhere in the world another tooth fell out.

Another family story that has endured (and I'm not certain if it isn't an exaggeration) is that my grandfather Little was such a stickler for table manners that, if his children displayed bad manners at a meal, he'd pick up a chair and throw it at them.

I do know that his drinking got in the way of what could have been a promising career in journalism. He was gifted with words and extremely funny. I have read several of his letters and they do not show a deb's delight so much as they reveal an attention to detail, an ability to know and describe people, and a charisma and charm that I imagine must have been hard to resist.

The idea of alcoholism as a disease was still a concept in its infant stages when my grandfather struggled with drinking. In spite of the fact that he did attend Alcoholics Anonymous meetings from time to time, I honestly believe his drinking was not a conscious decision so much as it was a runaway cancer. And so it did what alcohol addiction does when it is unchecked, it damaged his family and tragically cut short his life.

The children were not allowed to attend the funeral. They were informed of their father's death by Muv in the middle of a meal, quite out of the blue. She wouldn't accept tears because in her opinion, they were "better off without him." My mother, who was not more than nine years old when her father passed away, told me she "never believed Daddy was dead. Every day I'd walk up the street to meet his bus. I just didn't believe it."

❦ At the end of our trip to Creola, 'Tine and I accepted her childhood icons as lost. The mill pond may well have been right where she left it, but it was surrounded by oil fields and our exploration of the pond was barred by chained gates and mangled landscape.

So we left Creola, my grandmother anxious, as if she didn't want to linger too long at the scene of an accident, and we headed to a retirement village in Spanish Fort, fifteen miles north of Mobile, to see my great-aunt Everitt, my grandfather's sister.

In the dining hall of the home, I held my breath. From a distance I watched my great-aunt, supporting herself with a walker, move toward us. I admired her long regal face and the proud way she carried her tall thin frame. To me, she was a relic, like a single brick from a great monument. She had pretty snow-white hair that fell in curls over her deaf ears.

She smiled wanly at me. Writing on a tablet, she understood that I was Mary's daughter. I hoped to find through her some connection to the grandfather I never knew. But she had her own crowd she was sitting with and we did not seem important enough—her dead brother's wife and his granddaughter—to move for.

Instead, we sat in the dining hall with my Aunt Lil' Little and her daughter Anne, my grandfather's sister-in-law and niece. Anne couldn't tell me much about my grandfather no matter how much I prodded. I knew he was a drunk—that much had been written. Too, I knew he was charming, a real ladies' man.

"We are not a happy people," Anne said dolefully. I liked that phrase in spite of what it implied. *We are not a happy people*—as if our family merited a special line in history, like a small nation or a race.

These were the nice respectable kinfolk, the cousins who belonged on Mobile Mardi Gras courts. I had long savored the story about my grandfather's mother, Mamie, that illustrated her breeding, evident even in skinny times. Some of the gentry of Mobile were starting up a country club, and the founders went around soliciting membership among the well-to-do. When they stopped by Mamie's, her enthusiastic response to a paid social club was, "We have our friends."

My mother says I listen to stories with half an ear like everyone else in our family so I don't know how much hearing the untold stories would have mattered. My Aunt Everitt spoke to me finally on the way out of the assisted living home, in the lobby. She turned, glanced at my second cousin Anne and said, "I'm leaving *her* everything."

Knowing my temper has occasion to flare up, my grandmother brushed over the slight, an embarrassed look on her face. I know she wished she could hand me loving relatives with funny stories and charming photo albums. But this wasn't one of those times. I simply put my nose in the air, straightened my own tall frame, and said, "Really?"

Some weeks later, I got a letter from Anne. She spent time with my grandfather's sister, visiting at least weekly. In her letter she wrote that Aunt Everitt had repented, she hadn't meant to take it out on me—her relationship with my grandmother. She offered that I should come by with my mother Mary on my next trip to Mobile—she had a dinner ring she wanted to give her niece.

To me, the dinner ring sounded a lot like family jewels—of a Mary Everitt type. My mother was the last Mary Everitt until my poor sister Betsy got saddled with the name Mary Everitt Elizabeth Vance. Mom cheated a little by adding other names.

One Christmas my grandmother gave me a photograph of an oil painting family lore reputed to be in the Frick Collection in New York. It's a beautiful lively early- to mid-nineteenth-century portrait of the first Mary Everitt holding her first born, Augusta, a plump and rosy baby playing with a gold watch fob. The first Mary Everitt would have been my great-great-great-great grandmother. At least at that moment in her life, she looked like a duchess and I can't help but feel a certain awe, even from such a distance, that she is one of my direct ancestors. I am certain that was my grandmother's intent in giving me the photo.

Blue blood, fine connections—I wrote Anne back and told her there was no way I could understand all the family intrigues that happened before I was born, but I wanted to learn more about my grandfather, color in the image I had of him that was little more than the outline of a ghost. Feeling a fierce loyalty, I wrote Anne that, as for my grandmother, I was her granddaughter.

One of the things my grandmother was fond of saying was that in Atlanta it didn't matter where you came from, just where you were going. I guess after tangling with birthrights and Southern aristocracy, it must have felt good to her to be in a place where a person was recognized for his or her own worth.

✺ I was speculating with one of my cousins about where 'Tine's ashes might be scattered. Of course our uncle knew that she'd want them scattered at her birthplace at East Bay in Holley, Florida. My cousin and I commiserated. There was just so much time we'd missed out on, so many things we didn't know being the third generation. Partly because so much had happened before we were born and partly because we couldn't have that first-hand account that spouses and children get from a person. My mother and aunt and uncle knew 'Tine when she was truly young and struggling and making her way. We grandkids only knew her when she had come full circle in life, past childhood, marriages, triumphs, and heartaches. We never knew a time when 'Tine didn't know who she was, before she had come into the hard-won role of family matriarch.

But when the names are forgotten and the places of our ancestors are lost, the truth is, the past is never really behind us anyway.

CHAPTER THREE

My parents were so young when my brother Bird and I were born, they'd never really gotten much of an opportunity to grow up. I say this now, so many years later, after having had a child myself when I was only twenty. I can write about such things because I have had that same enigma ahead of me, in some ways I suppose I still do. Maybe it's not even growing up so much as it is *growing*. I think that is what my grandmother would say.

In 1976, at Thanksgiving at Sweet Apple, my father sent two one-way plane tickets to New Orleans—one for me and one for my little dog Greta. I was twelve years old. Bird was already with him. There's no need to hash over the old details now, but I will say that that Thanksgiving marked the beginning of my parent's divorce which was not truly behind me until I was twenty-one years old. Other than one short visit with my grandmother when I was fifteen, I did not see her for nine years. I didn't see or speak to my mother once in that same time, just short of a decade.

All those years, I secretly longed for my grandmother, even when I didn't miss anyone else. I missed her warmth and affection, the fact that with her, I could make mistakes and it wasn't the end of the world. In her book, right or wrong, a person could love someone no matter what they did.

Both sides of the family thought they were right but, of course, no one is ever entirely innocent, or entirely wrong. People are made up of so many things, the worst of which may be good intentions. My parents' divorce was about as public as a divorce can be. My grandmother ended up writing her 1981 novel, *Children My Children* based on what had happened to us—to *all* of us. 'Tine said, and I believe, that she wrote it to pay for the private detectives she'd hired to find us, to pay for lawyers' fees. Ever after, even when she knew the whole story, she would always say we had essentially been kidnaped. She just couldn't grasp the idea that we would not want to see her if we had the choice.

When I was cleaning out closets and gathering her papers for Emory University's archives, I had come across carbon copies of letters 'Tine had written to me and Bird when we were away. I had glanced at the content but was too emotionally wound up, working on two books, raising children, and trying to keep up with my grandmother to read them in their entirety. I mentioned them to her and she said I could do as I wished. So I'd tucked them away in a closet for later.

The fact that the letters resurfaced just after I lost my grandmother felt like an omen. I began to read over the words she had written, the lessons she wanted to teach us from so far away, the memories she willed us not to forget, and her battle to come to terms with losing us. It was as if I was reading them for the first time. Perhaps my father had given us the letters as they had come but if he did, I only remember having seen one or two.

Before our parents' divorce, me and my brother had been moved around from pillar to post, nearly a new home and a new school every year. Some years there would be more than one school and more that one home—we just never knew. We lived with our parents and also with my mother's sister, as well as with 'Tine for short periods.

My father was a jazz musician so at least some of the moving could be attributed to his profession. My mother started off fighting in the Civil Rights movement but she also worked as a book buyer, a carpenter, and at office jobs where I'm not sure what she did. A lot of the time, Daddy was on the road and I'm sure that at Mom's age, caring for two small needy children alone must have been overwhelming. She has always said she's done what she wanted with her life—eventually having six children in all—but I suspect she could have done anything she wanted that was in her will to do. She, like her father, is gifted with words, is witty, and possesses a kind of intelligence which did not pass down to me.

✣ The letter following—like all those below, one I found tucked away in the closet so long ago—was written to me while I was at Muv's house not long after she died, a month or so before I left to be with my father. At the time, I was trying to save money to buy a horse, a noble goal that I never attained. My brother said he thought when I grew up, I wouldn't marry for money, I'd marry for horses. As for me being a letter writer, 'Tine was always trying to encourage everyone in our family to write letters. I doubt I ever got a stamp on the one she describes.

'Tine writes about Larry and Walter in the letter. Larry Ashmead and Walter Mathews are inseparable friends. Larry was my grandmother's lifelong book editor and she followed him whenever he changed publishing houses, before he finally landed at HarperCollins, where he is today a vice president and senior editor. Walter was a business publisher and businessman in his own right—as 'Tine used to say, "He came from an old and stylish family in San Francisco." The truth is, whatever business connection she had with Larry, she loved him and Walter and counted them both among her dearest and closest friends. To me, they've always been sort of like distant uncles who live out of town and who have a sort of Santa Claus mystique about them. If you had asked 'Tine, she'd probably have said, "All good things—friendship, books, clothes, trips—come from Larry and Walter." To her, they did.

Angel, also mentioned in the letter, was a neighbor child in Alford for whom I babysat.

Friday, October 8, 1976

Dearest Sibley,

Your mother told me over the phone last night that you had written me a letter and, although it hasn't come yet, I am so pleased! I think of you all so much and long to hear from you. So it is very good to know somebody in the family is a letter-writer.

How are you liking school? And how is the horse fund coming? I walked down the road the other afternoon and the horses in the Wolffs' pasture asked about you. The weather here has been lovely—bright and cool, really too cool for swimming, although John and I tried it for a few minutes last weekend. You'll enjoy the lake on your next visit. Jack bought some pretty, really white sand and put it over that black stuff we put down and it looks like the ocean. Larry Ashmead took a deck chair and sat in the sun on it, calling it Lay-Me-Dune South. (Lay-Me-Dune is what he calls his ocean house, although Walter hates it.) Now the weather is gray and foggy and drippy, just right for staying indoors and writing, which is what I am going to be doing for the next two weeks. I took my vacation to work on my novel, Jincey, and I'd hate to sit at the type-writer if the weather was properly fallish and nice.

Tell your mother I am sending her a book called Eat and Stay Slim. *I don't think it can be done but she might figure it out. It does have exercises in the back and I have been doing them daily, in addition to walking a couple of miles. I am determined to get thin before Thanksgiving and to have a fine, flat tummy. I hate old ladies with big ugly stomachs, don't you?*

This is knitting weather and I am dying to get your sweater finished and off to you. Just a few more rows—unless you've grown a lot—and I can sew up the seams and send it on to you. I also need to finish Jack's and Uncle Jimmy's and then I'll be free to start something new. Did you take your big Christmas stocking with you? That would be a nice thing for you to knit for Angel, wouldn't it? If you're interested I'll send you the book with the pattern in it—or bring it at Thanksgiving when I come.

Meanwhile, be a sweet girl and write again.

Much love,

The picture she describes in the following letter was one I painted in watercolor on a scrap of lumber with a heart, flowers, a big present with a bow, and the words "I love you."

She kept it over her bed until she died.

The book she refers to is *Jincey*, published in 1978. The novel is set in Depression-era Mobile and is largely based on her childhood.

Thursday—Feb. 24, 1977

Dear Bird and Tib,

Somewhere between here and the Capitol there's a long letter to you all just waiting to be mailed. I wrote it over the weekend when John and Ted were here—all of us talking about you all and missing you—and then I couldn't find it when I got to the mailbox. Maybe some kind soul . . . but, no, it wasn't stamped.

. . . That book you thought I'd never finish last summer is due out in March. The stuff they're going to put on the jacket came out the other day. Your mother Xeroxed to send you a copy, not that you'll find it all that interesting, I'm afraid. Anyhow, it's done, except for the dedication which I still have to give them. I'm going to New York next week for the Pulitzer jury—you remember they asked me to serve when we were at Muv's?—so I'll drop the dedication off then.

Everything here reminds me of you all—your robe hanging in the bathroom, Tib, the painted board in the bedroom, the coffee mug you got me at McDonald's, Bird. Besides I've taken to dreaming of you nearly every night. Last night I dreamed one of those tiresome things where you can't get where you're going. I was in a motel looking for my room and there were seemingly endless rooms but none of them mine. Finally, feeling frustrated and sad, I sat down by a little table and suddenly you all were there, standing beside me. It was very real except that you all seemed somewhat younger and smaller.

. . . Time for my gallop down the road and then to work.

Much love from us all,

Snow, to which my grandmother refers in the following letter, was probably falling over the tiny town of New Harmony, Indiana, just as it was over 'Tine's cabin in Georgia. My brother and I lived in New Harmony off and on from 1976 to 1979 with my father's parents. The population of the town was and likely still is about eight hundred. A rare occurrence in the South, snow would settle on the ground in the Midwest for months at a time. It was one of the many things we loved about New Harmony. We built playhouse-size igloos and went sledding on a regular basis. The snow was deep enough to safely fall backwards onto and make snow angels.

Sweet Apple—1/13/78
Early in the morning

Dear Bird and Tib,

You've been on my mind daily although I haven't written lately. How are you all? Did you have a good Christmas? Did you get at least some of the things you were counting on? I'd love to hear from you and know for sure where you are and how you are.

We're having a touch of your kind of winter—snow, sleet, freezing rain. I came home early yesterday, built a beautiful fire, made a great casserole of lasagna and then took a walk in the snow with Richard Farrell, the 9-year-

old boy who lives in the Greens' house. Flakes were coming down thick and soft and beautiful and the dogs were wild with excitement. Even the ponies in the Wolffs' pasture seemed to enjoy it. The legislature started last Monday and I see your mother every day now. We had lunch together yesterday. Word at the office is that I won't be covering the House after the coming week. They are moving my column to the front of the section and want to give me more time for it. I'm not counting on it because all these decisions are subject to change and anyhow, after 20 years, I'd probably miss the to-do at the Capitol. In any case, I'm supposed to go to New York in March for the Pulitzer jury again.

. . . Daylight should be coming any minute now so I believe I'll stick on some clothes and go investigate the snow. It would be wonderful to be snowbound today but I just learned from my little weather radio that most of the roads are passable, if hazardous.

Do let me hear from you when you have a moment. I miss you and love you.

New Harmony is a historic town set on the Wabash River. It was founded in 1814 by people of Germanic background who called themselves Harmonists. Later Robert Owen used the town to conduct experiments in science and education. Many of the original buildings have been preserved and there are regular tours and lectures. Continuing in the tradition of culture and knowledge, there is a Roofless Church and memorials to Paul Tillich and Thomas Merton. Living there with our father's parents, we learned history, were baptized, and joined St. Stephens Episcopal Church which, along with its beautiful music, became a focus of our family and social lives.

My brother and I actually did teach 'Tine how to ride a bike. She was undaunted by the bloody scrapes that she received on her hands and knees almost every time she fell. I can still see her wobbling down the road by her house held up by determination and the belief that once you learn to ride a bike, you would never forget how.

Sweet Apple—Feb. 18, 1978

Dear Bird and Tib,

Awake at 3 A.M. thinking about you all so I decided to get up, put on the coffee pot and write to you. How are you and what are you up to these days? Are you still taking pictures, Bird? And have you learned to develop and print them? I hope so because I've always though that would be a lot of fun. I wish you would send me some pictures of you all so I can see how much you've grown. Why not take some with New Harmony backgrounds? I'd love to see that famous green labyrinthine garden, the log houses or any of the sights that make it such a pretty little town.

. . . It's almost gardening time but I don't have the greenhouse this year. Too expensive to heat it. And I may have to take off in April to finish my book so the muddy, dismal-looking old garden will have to wait, I'm afraid. Going to New York again for the Pulitzer jury March 1, and will stay the weekend for conferences with editors and a party Larry is giving. The most interesting plan to me is a walking tour of Greenwich Village. I've only had quick glimpses of it heretofore and know so little about its history and all the famous people, including Millay, who have lived and worked there. . . .

My latest enthusiasm is back packing. I'm dying to take it up but I can't generate much excitement in anybody here. . . . I want to do the Appalachian Trail before I get too old and decrepit to walk, sleep on the ground and skip my coffee. To get in condition I'm trying to stretch my morning hike a little bit more every day. Need you all to join me in this project. Remember how you taught me to ride a bike?

Time to let Fido up from his basement pad and get things going. How is Greta? Give her a pat for me. And do let me hear something from you all.

Much love from us all,

When I was in my late twenties, me and 'Tine went to New York for a Larry-and-Walter visit and I happily partook first-hand of the hospitality she mentions in the following letter written to my brother and me when Bird was fifteen and I was fourteen. The last meal we had on that trip, as I recall, was at yet another fancy restaurant. I picked up the menu and sighed. Larry asked what was wrong.

"I'm stuffed," I said.

"Why don't you order something light, then?" he suggested, "like the salmon?"

"I had the salmon for lunch," I replied. I've never felt so wonderfully decadent and taken care of since.

Anyway, me and 'Tine used to say that when I grew up we were going to have our own apartment in New York. If not there, then one of us would learn French and we'd move to Paris.

Later, 'Tine and I had opportunities to enjoy together the kind of special lunch in the office of Tine's long-time friend

Amelia Smith that 'Tine describes in the letter below. These lunches often included Dorothy Spence, executive director of the Atlanta chapter of the American Institute of Architects and state legislator Grace Towns Hamilton and her sister Harriet, all of whom have passed away by now. By the time me and 'Tine were going there together, the occasion of visiting the Capitol had become more like old home day.

March 7, 1978

Dearest Bird and Tib,

The mailbox robber has struck again! Came back from five days in New York and there was no letter from you all. Just bills and junk, darn it.

How are you? How is school? Have you kept well? What are you doing with yourselves? Have you received letters, books, money and other stuff from me or is everything lost in a snowdrift somewhere? How about some pictures?

The time in New York was lovely. Stayed at the Algonquin, the famous old hotel where hundreds of writers have lived and worked, for two nights and then Walter Mathews moved over to Larry's and gave us his apartment for two nights. They are marvelous hosts and when I wasn't working on the Pulitzer entries up at Columbia University, they had theatre tickets, asked us out to dinner, gave a party and took us sightseeing. I came home utterly exhausted but, in a way, refreshed too. It was profitable, too, to see and talk with all my editors and I got an agent for the first time since I've been writing books. Larry recommended him strongly and says I need somebody to look after money arrangements, which I'm sure is true.

. . . Your mother has been working long hours at the legislature. She insisted that I come over for lunch yesterday and I went, although I have been shy about seeing my old pals in the House since I'm not covering the General Assembly any more. We ate fried chicken and little biscuits and wonderful Cloudt's salad in Amelia Smith's office (Remember her? She's your mother's immediate boss.) There were about a dozen of us, including some members, and I enjoyed it very much. But just as I was thinking about getting my coat and leaving, the House reconvened and about 10 members arrived. They said they wanted me to visit them on the floor and I said I couldn't, I hadn't brought my floor pass. "Come along," they said, taking me by the arm, and the next thing I knew I was walking down the main aisle and all the members were standing and applauding. They had flowers for me, passed a resolution and came up to shake my hand and pose for pictures. (Terrible pictures of me, I'm sure, because I was crying.) I still haven't recovered from it.

The legislature adjourned last night. I don't know what time because after the day's work and excitements I came home, cooked supper and died. . . .

This has been a long one but I haven't written in a couple of weeks and I had so much to tell you. Now you all get busy and tell me something. I wonder about you all the time, miss you and love you very much.

The Golden Age bus never did come as she predicted in the following letter. She never stopped walking, working, or going to the newspaper. She also mentions *Jincey,* which she considered her best work, as do many others. She spent ten years

is little-known book, and many more thinking
Jincey was largely biographical, she said it wasn't
could have published when Muv was alive—
the bigamy and personal details.

1978

d and Tib,

*morning and I have to catch the bus in an
hour but I have been assembling some magazines for you
and thought I'd write a quickie to go with them. They are
mostly things Larry sends, except for the Sunday* Journal-
Constitution Magazine, *which I am sending because it
has a rather interesting piece on back-packing by my old
friend Phil Garner. . . . The way things are going I may not
get to hit the trail until the Golden Age bus comes to get
me. Can't find any young companions! . . .*

*It looks like my little yellow car has finally quit. Jack says
it isn't safe for me to drive it any longer—some major matter about brake drums—and we didn't even get a tag for it
this year. I am currently driving the truck into Roswell and
catching the bus. If and when I get book money I suppose
I'll have to buy a new car and I hate flinging money down
that rat hole, as you know. I wrote you that I finished
Jincey, I believe, and now I'm all but walking the floor
waiting for the verdict. My editor at Simon & Schuster told
me to expect about a two-week delay because she does most
of her long book reading on weekends. (This one is 510
pages.) She probably got it yesterday—at the earliest—and
I may be a basket case before I hear. . . . I promise you this*

is the first time I've acted this vaporish and idiotic over a book. . . . Retiring has been on my mind a lot lately. It would be a few years early but I wouldn't lose much money by stopping work now and there's a lot I'd love to be doing. However, they gave me a raise yesterday and urged me to stay so I suppose I'll have to—for a while anyhow. I have another book my editors are interested in and I'd love time off. Do write to me. I love you.

I don't think my grandmother ever cared if we became famous or financially successful adults just as long as we were "happy and useful" ones. The reference below to my "bird-house feeder" is evocative of my early life with 'Tine—so much simply happened in her yard, as if it were an open-air playroom.

June 15, 1978

Dear Bird and Tib,

Your birthdays are coming up and I think about you a lot and wish I could write you a letter which would help you along the road to becoming happy and useful adults. As old as I am, you'd think I might have picked up some wisdom to pass on to my dearly beloved grandchildren. I'm not sure that I have learned anything to ease the pains that life brings. I guess they are essential to living and something we can learn from. I have learned something about being happy and that's a high respect for truth and love.

But maybe we have to learn our own lessons as we go along and nothing I say to you now will mean anything to

*you until you learn it from firsthand experience. Anyhow,
know that I think of you at every minute of every day,
almost, with much love and long to see you.*

*Late yesterday I got back from St. Simons Island, where
I had to make a speech Tuesday night. The trip down on
Air South was an experience. We were about 100 miles out
of Atlanta and a tide of lavender liquid started flowing
down the aisle. I heard the young mother across the aisle
say to her children, "That's not Kool-Aid, that's water."
Then the stewardess came and said, "No smoking, no
smoking! We're losing hydraulic fluid!" In a little while the
pilot came on the intercom and told us the plane was "dis-
abled" and we were turning back to Atlanta. I wasn't particularly concerned until I started thinking that hydraulic
fluid is necessary to brakes and maybe to putting the
wheels down. "Oh, boy," I thought, "we're going to do a
belly-buster!" But we landed all right and the worst of it
was an hour-and-a-half wait for another plane. I got to
Epworth-by-the Sea in time to make my speech—9
o'clock and tired!—and then I spent the night with our
old friends, Mary and Tom Gash.*

*. . . After two weekends of hard work on it—I have a
blister on my hand as big as a quarter!—the yard is beginning to shape up. I have a lot of pink and red geraniums in
the window boxes and barrels and tubs and they are
blooming their heads off. Your birdhouse-feeder, Sibley,
was on the ground when I went out one morning and I
hurried to see why. The branch of the peach tree where
you put it had broken. So it's in the crotch of the apple tree
now and I spread seeds on its little front porch when I
have a minute. The four-o'clocks we planted by the front
chimney, Bird—remember that day?—are coming back.*

The ground is hard and dry there but I spread good cow doo and watered it in and I expect them to flourish.

It's time to get to the office so I'll stop and mail this on the way. Larry sent these pictures he took last month. Thought you might like to have them.

Much love to you both,

So many of my childhood books were lost to overnight moves and crossing state lines. What books we had that weren't signed by their authors, we pasted bookplates in, wrote our names in, and in general, claimed unwavering ownership of. I was fifteen years old when 'Tine wrote the letter below. The same year, she came for a brief visit to New Harmony—the only one while we were away. I was no longer the little girl who built birdhouses and hung them from the high boughs of trees. I was big—as tall as she was, but teenagery plump and awkward. We picked up where we left off, laying down together in bed, snuggling as if the previous three years apart had been a minor glitch in the greater field of time.

David Vance is my little half-brother who was born while we were away. I hate the thought that I missed his baby years as I did John-Stephen's, who came into the world a year after David. There's a fifteen-year difference between David and me and a twenty-one-year difference between me and my little sister Betsy Vance, who was born shortly before I came back to Atlanta.

Wednesday, February 20, 1980
Sweet Apple

Dearest Bird and Tib,

Missed Monday. Terrible cold and much work but I thought of you all a lot and sent loving vibes in that direction anyhow. Did you get your valentines? Did you have a happy day? I hope so.

By now I figured I was past the valentine stage but no, I was rich in them. I had to make a speech at the Plaza Thursday night where they honored Mr. Ben Fortson, the wonderful old secretary of state, posthumously with the annual Big Heart award. There were 12 of us to make brief and, they hoped, light speeches, including all the governors. I sat next to former Gov. Ellis Arnall and had a fine time and when I got to Candler Street to spend the night, your mother had my bed turned down, my nighties and slippers laid out and TWO valentines on my pillow. One from David was fat with pictures. She said she sent you all some, too.

. . . Leslie Bridges (remember her, your mother's British friend?) moved back to England, taking her babies who reminded me so much of you two at their age, with her. She told your mother she could have anything left in the house, one of those big, beautiful old houses on Fourteenth Street. We went over there Friday afternoon and wandered through and it was mostly sad old left-behinds but I saw a copy of The Yearling *on the floor and picked it up and opened it. Guess what, it was inscribed "Sibley Fleming." We stood there looking at it and both of us were near tears. It was like your hand had reached out and touched us, Tib. Your mother has the book now, if you want it.*

Up at 3 a.m. to work on the new novel so I'd better get at it. Larry's coming in March for something at Emory but is going to spend the weekend here and I need to have a nice chunk of manuscript for him to see. I have to sand-wich the novel in between work at the office, work at home and speeches (one Saturday at the Historical Society, one tomorrow at the University of Georgia.)

Thinking of you, wishing I could see you, hear from you, touch you.

Much, much love from us all,

The letter below was written at the time that the suburbs began encroaching on Sweet Apple. In spite of the fact that houses eventually were built all around her, my grandmother still went about her life as if she were hidden deep in the woods. Brookfield West was the first subdivision to be built near her cabin.

March 3, 1980—Sweet Apple

Dearest Bird and Tib,

It's 4 A.M. and I have been up a couple of hours drink-ing coffee and admiring the moonlight on a perfectly stun-ning snowfall. The thermometer says 10 degrees and I keep turning on faucets and flushing toilets, hoping to keep the water running—at least until I can get a go-to-work-bath. IF I can go to work. The roads were iced over yesterday and hazardous, they kept assuring us over the radio.

How are you all? Are you having WEATHER too? If so, I hope you're not making those basketball and flute jun-kets to far places but are staying in, snug and warm. . . . My only expedition yesterday was to the mailbox. Church was canceled. Stranger and I wobbled down the road together, trying to avoid slipping and sliding on the ice which seems to have coated everything before the snow started falling. He's a crazy dog (Clyde's puppy, you remember) and goes absolutely wild when there's snow, leaping and barking about and nipping at my jacket and running in circles. Birds flocked to the feeder in droves and Fido, the cat, came in from wherever he goes for weeks at the time. (I suspect Brookfield West, he's so sleek and fat). I slept a lot to make up for late hours I've been keeping and it must have done me good because I'm ready to tackle old Monday morning with renewed vigor this morning.

My grandmother said when she was a young working mother, she reserved many a Sunday evening for dressmaking. She could whip up a new outfit for about a dollar then. This habit, continued over into our childhood with bright simple sun suits and dresses without too many ruffles—she must have gotten better at ruffling by the time David came along.

Euell Gibbons was a favorite naturalist of all three of us— my grandmother, brother, and me. We loved eating daylillies battered and fried and got a kick out of spoofing Gibbons's once-popular commercial for Grape Nuts cereal—we called it Grape *Guts.*

At the end of the following letter she refers to my half-brother David and his family, the Vances, who are my mother's second family.

April 10, 1980—Sweet Apple

Dear Bird and Tib,

Here I am back from my travels and thinking of you two. Did you have a happy Easter? . . . Dog Island was beautiful. We had a cottage on the bay side with an almost all-glass front and a wonderful view of the dunes with twisted, bonsai-looking oaks and the beach and water beyond. All the sunsets on the bay side seem to be spectacular, making us a little sorry that our lot is on the gulf side. But not too sorry because it is a beautiful lot and since the Nature Conservancy is buying most of the island, including the lots behind us and in front of us, we won't be crowded, if and when we get a house there. The morning we stopped for breakfast at Panacea (sent you cards from there, remember?), a builder we have been trying to find showed up, sat with us, took our plans off and is supposed to give us an estimate soon. He is well thought of in the area, reliable, etc., so we hope. . . . If you are still interested in Euell Gibbons-type food, Bird, you would have enjoyed that lunch. Another pilot and his wife were there and they had gathered wild mushrooms and the tips of smilax and prepared them for us. The smilax tips, boiled and buttered, tasted almost exactly like asparagus.

Sibley, you provided a darling Easter suit for David. He looked so adorable in the blue jumper and white ruffled blouse I made him for Christmas I decided at the last minute that he needed a yellow suit for Easter. I thought I had some yellow linen I bought years ago to make myself a dress but I couldn't find it. Rooting around in boxes and trunks I came upon a yellow shift I almost finished for you when you were about ten. (Remember, with the different colored pockets?) I ripped it up, pressed it and made David a little jumper in about two hours. They go to the Quaker church in Druid Hills and he must have looked like a goldfinch or a daffodil.

The column 'Tine wrote about hand-me-downs was without a doubt one of the truest stories she ever wrote in regards to my feelings. It wasn't just hand-me-downs that I objected to, it was thrift stores and clothes that had been out of fashion for two decades. She thought in terms of respectably covering my poor little body and believed there really was a timelessness about red plaid, black velvet ribbons, and old pea jackets. I thought I never would have anything new but then, of course, I did. I got new things and then I grew up and bought new and learned the wisdom of hand-me-downs firsthand.

'Tine's book, *Small Blessings*, published in 1976, was written on the screen porch of Muv's Florida house the summer that Muv died.

Sweet Apple-January 21, 1980

Dearest Bird and Tib,

Here it is 4:30 A.M. and I have had many cups of coffee, checked over the seed catalogues, built a fire in the fireplace, put a loaf of whole-wheat bread to rise, set the table and . . . whew! . . . I'm ready to write to my babies. How in the world are you? Are you busy at school, having fun, helping around the house, babysitting, singing, playing, even THINKING about writing your old granny? Gosh, I'd love a letter! Or even, as we used to say, a penny postcard.

Did you get the big box of hand-me-downs, Tib? The next box will be yours, Bird, but not hand-me-downs because I don't seem to get boy things. I do have a nice gray suede jacket Walter Mathews sent but it needs cleaning, which would be horrendously expensive, and then I'm not sure it would fit or that you would like it. Sibley, the long tweed skirt went to some of the inaugural parties in Washington when the Carters went into office. It was bitter cold, as you may remember, and I was so glad to have a warm skirt for the evening things. I hope you can get some use out of it. Incidentally, did you ever read the Good Housekeeping *magazine story about you and hand-me-downs? It was a chapter from* Small Blessings *and the magazine paid me $500 for it. My editor, Carolyn Blakemore, said it was her favorite chapter in the book. If you didn't get it and would like to see it, I'll send you a copy.*

The letter following tickles me because 'Tine absolutely hated, disdained, feared, and did not comprehend television. She had one in her room which Jack watched but it held so little attraction for her that she could read through all but the most riveting news items.

August 16, 1980

Dearest Bird and Tib,

Cool and dark here at 6:30 A.M. and I have been prowling around drinking coffee and thinking of you all. Have you had a good summer? Are you ready for school to start? Will you be going back to New Harmony this year? Do write and let me know all.

. . . My television performance on election night, as awkward and ugly as it was, must have been all right

*because they have asked me back for the run-off on the
night of August 26. I dread it because television's so visual
and I'm so un-visual but the money will come in handy so
I accepted. It's too late to get my face lifted but I'm thinking about a new hair-do, losing 10 pounds and buying
some pancake makeup. What do you think, Sibley?*

*Send me some pictures, Bird. I have the two beauties
you took of Sibley playing the flute in that lovely open-air
church in New Harmony in a double frame here on my
desk. (Also have John Steven and David in a single
frame.) You and Ted are scarce items in my photo gallery
and I have a sudden urge to round it out and update it. I'd
like to update the measurements on the door facing in the
kitchen, too, but I have to have your physical presence for
that. Will you ever come and see me again? I hope and pray.*

Now to start the day. Much, much love to you both,

*P.S. David now says 'Tine as plain as Mama, Daddy and
Bebe (baby.)*

In the letter following, my grandmother writes again of family photographs. She was constantly digging around for old
black frames, and moving pictures around from room to room
and from wall to wall. It was her belief that it was necessary to
re-hang pictures in order for them to hold your attention.

Roy Wyatt, mentioned in the letter, was an old friend and
a garden writer for the *AJC.*

Sept. 22, 1980

Dear Bird and Tib,

. . . This morning at nine o'clock a camera team from WSB is coming out to do a columnist-at-home show and you all know what a whirlwind cleaning jag I've been on. I didn't know they were coming until Thursday night and I have mopped and scrubbed, mowed and planted up a storm. The yard looks pretty. Roy Wyatt gave me a bargain on some chrysanthemums to enliven the droopy border along the rock wall. I moved the big pie safe out of the living room into the kitchen, to replace the little one which is falling to pieces. (Ron is going to re-glue it for me.) In the move I found the little jar you used to keep coins in, Tib. It still has some in it. I didn't open it but stood a minute thinking about you and missing you and then I put it back.

Before I got on the cleaning jag and could be more leisurely I filled one of those big frames with snapshots of you all and that was fun. I went through my supply and Muv's, picking pictures which would fit into the little squares, circles and rectangles that are pre-cut in the mat. Across the top I have a shot of the four of you taken at Sibley's birthday party across the river, Bird in his sailor suit at about three years, the four of you playing with wooden swords by the rock wall in the backyard. . . . I enjoyed looking at all the pictures so much I'm going on a framing spree and put many, many more where I can see them. How about some new ones, Bird?

It's just a little after 3 a.m. and I've been up about two hours, puttering around. I'll be dead tired by the time the WSB folks arrive and so glad when that is over. It's nice of them to include me in their series but I do love time to poke around working in the yard, taking walks, etc. Our turnip patch is flourishing. We had our first mess of greens for din-

*ner yesterday and still get enough tomatoes to keep us going.
They're small at this time of year but wonderfully tasty.*

By the time the letter below was written, Bird and I were
living in Shreveport, Louisiana, with our father. We moved in
with him so that we could spend our last year before adulthood together. The Billy she mentions in the letter was Jack's
Cajun cousin, Billy Waters. Rosemary was Billy's wife. I was
seriously studying classical flute and my brother was finishing high school. It turned out to be my last year in high
school as well and the last year my brother and I would live
together after so many in which we had been the stable factor
in each other's lives.

October 22, 1980

Dearest Bird and Tib,

*Out of touch a while and I really miss writing to you
as well as hearing from you. There's been so much going
on here. You may have heard about the nursery school
explosion which killed a teacher and five little black children last week? I had to cover that and have been busy
since getting things at home ready for the fall, leaf-look-
ing trip of Billy and Rosemary. The house is so clean I
just roam around admiring it but if they don't hurry it'll
all be to do over again. They were due Saturday, had
unexpected foreign visitors to arrive, and may finally get
here tonight (Wednesday). I have a great bag of mustard
and turnip greens picked and washed ready to cook.
They're out of our garden and the nicest, cleanest,
crispest we ever had. Also have an apple pie cooling on*

the meat block and a ham cooked, all in case I'm delayed at the office today.

. . . Children are so valuable in this life. Trouble and grief sometimes, of course, but pure delight and pleasure and comfort and joy most of the time. What kind of life would I have had without my children and grandchildren? For one thing children expand you so.

. . . We're having beautiful weather. My chrysanthemums have been almost showy. The maple trees are at their splendid best. The days are bright and warm, the nights blanket and fireplace cool. I know it's time to bring in the geraniums, begonias and sultanas but I hate to strip the yard so early. Still I have my pots ready in the red wagon. (Had to buy a new one, children. The one we bought finally wore out.)

In some ways my grandmother did go on with her life. She began building the house on Dog Island, and continued raising more grandchildren. My brother returned home for visits during his first year in college. There was finally calm—the constant clamor of crisis had died down to a distant echo of the past.

As for me, my last year in high school was my junior year. I was already making money with my flute, playing in small orchestras, chamber ensembles, and the Shreveport Youth Orchestra at Centenary College. So, when it came time for Bird, who is nearly a year older than I (as I like to remind him, he is eleven months, one week, and six days older), to start applying for colleges, I took my tests to get out of high school, auditioned for scholarships, applied for grants and loans, and got into Centenary.

My major was music performance but I later changed to pre-med. An old college friend once said to me, "Even at that age, Sibley, you seemed so on your own, so responsible for yourself, I'm sure that's why we connected." For the most part, I spent my idle college hours writing spider poems in my invertebrate classes and staying up late writing songs about lost love and small vignettes as fleeting as that which is glimpsed out of the corner of the eye.

I was in college when 'Tine wrote the following letter to me and I don't know where she would have sent it. It wasn't until after she died that I read the words, crying and remembering how much we truly loved each other.

Sweet Apple—October 29, 1981

Dearest Tib,

The other day I was dusting and rearranging books and a sheaf of pressed leaves fell out of one. The leaves you and I put there on a bright fall day five years ago! I sat on the floor and bawled like a fool, remembering the day, the little girl you were, your eagerness to learn the names of the trees and our love for each other.

. . . The fall here has been spectacular. Billy and Rosemary came last week and took us on a swing to the Smokies to see the leaves. We picnicked beside Amicalola Falls and spent a night in Gatlinburg and then home to rain, which we badly needed, and long sessions by the fire. I made an apple pie and gathered and cooked turnip greens out of the garden yesterday, barely able to keep my eyes off the maples, sweetgums and dogwood, which are

glorious. We're going to have Thanksgiving dinner at your mother's new house—a really pretty old house, which you would love. Bird is coming and it would be wonderful if you'd come, too. . . . David and John Steven know you from your pictures and they would be ecstatic to have a big sister. David refers to Bird as "my big brudder."

Do let us hear from you, dear Tib. We love you very much.

My college career was cut short when I left with two friends—Patrick Hurley, an Irish-Cypriot; and Satbirsing Bhatia, a native of Bombay—to make our fortune in the poverty-stricken country of Ireland. Patrick's father gave us the job of running a vacation pub by the sea in southern Cork next to a castle which he also owned. It was there I met and married Norbert Schaum, a Berliner who had moved to Ireland to do his art work.

Our son Vincent was born in St. Finbarr's Hospital in Cork City on April 22, 1985. Four months later, with baby, flute, guitar, and typewriter—I'd begun what I thought might be a first novel, terrible work—I headed back to the United States, to Santa Barbara, California. Our marriage was probably doomed from the beginning—I was much too young to know who or what I wanted.

An art curator once commented on a copy of a Rembrandt that Norbert had made, momentarily fooled. Norbert responded, "I can't afford a Rembrandt so I have to paint my own." In spite of the fact that he was the most gifted artist and sculptor I've ever known, we divorced shortly after our second son was born. Still, I can't help but respect his innate talent.

It was in Santa Barbara, late one night, feeling nostalgic and homesick, I called 'Tine for the first time since I was twelve. A few days later, I was surprised to find a cheerful package of books and a letter from her in the mailbox.

❧ It wasn't easy to figure how to go back home after so much fighting, after so much had been said, so many stands had been taken. Secretly, after I was living in Ireland and was married, I harbored the dream that I'd write and publish the Great American Novel and that my grandmother and mother would read it and all would be forgiven. At twenty-one, I was too young to understand the pain they'd gone through. I only understood my own. The fact was that I was already forgiven. It might be hard to go home but the door was always open.

CHAPTER FOUR

Over the years my grandmother had many assistants to help keep her schedule and answer mail. Perhaps a habit or, more likely, just not wanting to miss anything, she always preferred to answer the phone herself. It had a signature lilt, even when she was down—"Celestine Sib-leey!"—hanging on the final vowel like a high note in a show tune.

She was the fastest writer I've ever known and was probably the fastest the newsroom has ever known. She didn't think—she wrote. I've seen her work on news stories outside of her column, taking notes and doing a bit of research and turning it into a full-blown article within the space of an hour. And to her, she was lagging behind.

One day in 1987 when I was working as her assistant we'd gone out cavorting, frankly, in downtown Atlanta—shopping for white dishcloths at Kessler's department store, eating turnip greens and cornbread at Woolworth's. We returned past her deadline.

Her editor, a young woman and new to my grandmother, cornered her immediately, frantic. "Where's your column? It's late! I need it now!"

There are moments when you are proud of your elders and this was one of them. My grandmother turned calmly, her eyes scanning the editor, then, with some annoyance, she said, "Can you give me *five* minutes?"

Five minutes later, the column was done.

My grandmother marked time with me and my brother Bird as the periods *before they left* (before our parents' divorce and our father subsequently taking us to live with him and our paternal grandparents), *while they were away* (the period from 1976 to 1985), and *after they returned* (the time from 1985 to her death in 1999). My short life had been lived so chaotically. Up until Vincent was born in 1985, events had passed so quickly and were so irretrievably out of control, I had taken to saying that I was born the day after I was conceived. All of the moving with our young parents in our early childhood; the drawn-out divorce over which our family was torn apart; getting through three years of college on my own; marital strife and moving with four-month-old Vincent to Santa Barbara; then reuniting with Norbert (who stayed in Ireland for six months before joining me to drive across America in a VW bus with our new baby); and returning to a family which had been torn from my life nine years previous.

In 1986, my grandmother hired me as her assistant at the *AJC*. I have no doubt in my mind that I was the worst, least effective assistant 'Tine had ever had. There was always more Wite-Out than ink on my letters. Still, she'd approve them good-humoredly and toss them into the outgoing mail. Knowing no employer is that blind, I also have no doubt that she gave me the job so that we could make up for lost time together. We made up for those missing years on a daily basis. My salary came to about one hundred dollars a week, enough for my train fare and child care for Vincent. He was just a baby, a little under two years old.

My work consisted mostly of straightening up her office. Since my position had been vacant for some time, there were boxes of unanswered mail. Being no paperwork guru, they simply looked better to me in the trash than they did underfoot. I just threw things out, which horrified 'Tine, the Head Pack Rat. Once her column was done, if she had phone calls to make, she'd send me out for some coffee and a treat, a "goodie" as she referred to anything sweet outside of a meal.

We'd talk. She'd want to know how Vincent was and then marvel at whatever small, babyish thing he'd done in the past twenty-four hours.

"I believe he's the prettiest child we got," she'd say, while also being complimentary about him not sleeping or throwing a tantrum, cooing over his having the intelligence to build a castle out of wooden blocks as if he'd invented all of it. Probably since her own children were small, she'd always talked about having even one of the boys in our family attend Harvard. "Vincent may be the one," she'd say. Of course, she wasn't singling him out, she actually said that about all the males in our family.

I was only twenty-two. I was thinking I wanted to go back to college and finish school myself. I shared my darkest feelings about having thrown away my life by getting married and having a baby too young, how it seemed that there was nothing left for me.

"You just had six children too few," she'd say, "if you'd just had six more then they could take care of the one."

I don't know how she would have felt about it if I taken her advice literally. But she was adamant about the fact that children do not take from your life, they add to it more than any college degree or accomplishment. "Draw from your experience. You can learn so much from your children," she said. "I did from mine."

She essentially had been a single mother and had taken care of her children and had held down a job. Not that she took any credit for all the juggling or struggle, to her it was more like, you see your duty and you do the best you can. When you wake up every day, no matter how overwhelming or how much life is throwing at you, you simply accept that you do what you can in any given moment and then just do it.

Working as her assistant was more like getting an education than laboring, anyhow. We ate Barker's hot dogs in Woodruff Park, ducked into the now-defunct Herron's restaurant for sumptuous occasions and filled our veins and our souls with grease from the Varsity drive-in. We visited art exhibits and took walks on the city sidewalks, stopping to talk to vendors or for her to fish deep down in the bottom of her purse for money to give a beggar. They always asked for money for a meal in spite of the fact that food could be had for free at any of the numerous shelters downtown.

I mentioned this to her, that she wasn't feeding anyone by handing out her spare change—she was buying rounds of drinks. She told me she knew that. When she'd been younger and more full of herself, a poor man in ragged clothes had asked for some change for breakfast. She explained how she'd gotten that do-gooder mentality and told the man that she'd be glad to take him to breakfast. She did, but he couldn't eat the eggs or grits she'd paid for and when he told her the truth—that all he'd wanted was a bottle—she was ashamed that she'd begrudged him the one small comfort that would have made his life more bearable. After that, she said, she didn't take street people to breakfast, but she didn't stop giving money either.

One day I was approached by one of the old reporters at the *AJC* with a sort of undercover job. I'd chauffeur him to his stories and get an education while I watched him work. The only requirement was that I keep the job secret. Above all, I was admonished not to tell my grandmother. She wouldn't approve, he was pretty certain.

I was beside myself. Although I was married with a baby, I was hardly grown or mature. I was so flattered, to be asked out in the adult world by a crusty old reporter hitting all the hard news spots—maybe even murder sites, I could only hope.

I did not tell my grandmother *all* but I did tell her part of the truth about my new job and she was not impressed. It didn't take much for her to piece together my handshake deal and, after that, it just wasn't an option.

"You have to be careful who you befriend because people will judge you by the company you keep," she told me protectively.

"What about the company *you* keep?" I asked. This was not the grandmother who didn't care what anyone thought. Half her friends were on the street or in jail. In fact, prisoner letters were her favorite—they came with a marking on the outside of the envelope stating clearly they were from folks who were incarcerated. She'd want to help them—they were all so innocent. She'd read every line and then she'd make a call to someone such as Wayne Snow, head of the state of Georgia's parole board, and ask if anything could be done. Come to think of it, she loved convicts almost as much as she loved politicians. I told her so.

"Well, when you are my age, you can keep company with whoever you choose. On a young girl, they judge. On an old woman, they think *eccentric*."

"How about I be an eccentric young girl?" I asked.

No dice. I don't know what happened to the reporter and I guess I'm sorry I never got to take the job. Maybe she was right but I doubt she gave me advice that she would have taken herself. Such is life.

✂ My grandmother wasn't always confident. She'd survived so many regimes at the newspaper, so many years, people coming and going, attitudes and wants changing, that she was always on the alert, careful to appreciate her position.

She kept a folder of letters upon the suggestion of her second husband Jack. It was called the "You're a good guy, Jack Strong" folder and it was where we kept all the admiring acclamations that could be shown to a potential angry employer.

There was a shake-up at the paper back in the mid-1980s. A bunch of the old guard left and the new replacement to head up the features department was Dudley Clendinen from *The New York Times*. Friends would come into 'Tine's office to report what they knew, secretively, as if anything that goes on in a newsroom could ever be kept under wraps.

The new boss opened his shop by asking her to lunch, an invitation she interpreted with doom. He wanted to take her to the Ritz-Carlton.

"People get fired at the Ritz," she said to me, furrowing her brow. She hadn't come so far and worked so hard to be taken to the Ritz.

She followed a plan. When Mr. Clendinen came to get her, she was her most charming ingratiating self. They got out of the newspaper building and she suggested that they go to

Woolworth's instead of the Ritz, her reasoning being that no one ever got fired at Woolworth's.

"My dear woman . . . ," he said something to that effect with exasperation, and insisted on the Ritz.

To slow the journey to her death—which was what my grandmother would have considered being fired—she stopped along the way to rouse street people on the sidewalks from their slumber.

"Are you okay?" she asked with concern. This bit of show-manship was not only to bide time but to show her humanitarian interests. How could someone fire a woman who was so obviously compassionate? Why, it'd be *wrong*.

Mr. Clendinen did get 'Tine to the Ritz—eventually—but he didn't fire her. He changed her column from six times a week to four times a week, with the columns running in both the *Journal* and the *Constitution*. You might consider it a promotion even.

❧ Around about the same time, we had an invitation to lunch at the governor's mansion. We were asked by no less than the governor's wife herself, Elizabeth Harris. 'Tine and the first lady had been been on campaign trails together—Mrs. Harris working for her husband, Joe Frank, and my grandmother, of course, covering the election for the paper. 'Tine said Mrs. Harris wanted to meet me.

My grandmother had confided in her about how she'd missed my brother and me when we were gone and Mrs. Harris had promised to pray for our return. The lunch, I believe, was for me to get to go the governor's mansion—a treat—and for my grandmother to show the state's first lady that all the prayers that had gone floating heaven-bound had been answered.

As I recall, when we drove through the security gate of the executive mansion of Georgia, the guard recognized my grandmother easily, we parked, and walked directly to the front door. The house is in the expected Greek Revival style—two-story, thick white columns, red brick—and is surrounded by expansive green lawns with azaleas and magnolias, almost like a movie set. We rang the doorbell and a staff lady answered, directing us to the library to wait.

We might have been in a favorite museum, my grandmother was so familiar with the surroundings. She went over the bookshelves pointing out how the governor's library housed books by Georgia writers and books about Georgia. She looked for her own titles and made jokes.

Moments later Mrs. Harris arrived, out of breath, taking off a straw gardening hat, shifting her clippers to her left hand so she could greet us.

"Are the clippers props or were you really out working in the garden?" my grandmother asked congenially.

"Celestine! I really *was* out cutting flowers," she smiled looking at me. "And this is Sibley? I'm so glad to finally meet you," she said with familiarity, as if somehow our paths had crossed before.

The rest of the lunch was spent in the little breakfast room by the kitchen, one chef for three women. It might have been a lunch party at the home of my grandmother or any other of her friends and there was no doubt, I was there to look at. They chatted happily, including me in the conversation every now and then.

Before we left, Mrs. Harris hugged me warmly and said, "Do you know I never stopped praying that you would come home?" My grandmother stood by watching, content.

⅍ One day, Japanese TV news reporters called my grandmother at her office and said they wanted to interview her. She was not impressed. I couldn't understand it.

"Remember Pearl Harbor," she said, puncturing the air with her long index finger. And then she gathered her witnesses, people of her generation in the newsroom, and asked them if they didn't agree. Of course they did. (The appearance was that everyone always agreed with my grandmother, but I'm not so sure that that was the case as much as it was that she was just always careful to solicit the opinions of like-minded persons.)

But it wasn't just the Japanese, per se, it was television itself which gave my grandmother pause. Following one TV interview long after I had stopped working as her assistant, I got a call from a bedraggled publicist who had been put through the ringer with my grandmother's less than congenial behavior. Apparently, 'Tine had objected to arriving at the television studio only to learn that she wouldn't be appearing on the show for another hour. She didn't like being held in the wings while others were interviewed, as if her time weren't as valuable as the TV people's time.

In a loud and carrying voice, she commented on the interviewer. "Doesn't he have pretty teeth?" she crooned. "Isn't he an attractive young man? I don't understand why he doesn't get a real job, like driving a truck or digging ditches."

⅍ As I grew into young adulthood, I discovered that people would befriend me to try to get my grandmother to do something, that is to write a column to support whatever cause they were touting. What they didn't know was that the best way to get her *not* to write a column, make a speech, or show up somewhere, was to try to try to get to her through a family member, truly it was the kiss of death. Any relation of a media employee knows what I'm talking about. The first time it happens, you feel a little used. After a while, it just seems silly—the lengths people will go to for publicity. Eventually you realize it's part of the territory.

Not that 'Tine didn't allow her column to spill over into her personal life. When she couldn't get her way with one of us, she'd employ her column to boost *her* cause. She was stubborn like that and she wasn't beneath posting our family differences in the newspaper and leaving them for her readers to decide.

Before Wolfie was born, in 1990, she played hell in her column, garnering support from probably half the grandmothers in Georgia—how could I name a child something so harsh as *Wolfgang?* What kind of teasing would he endure on an American playground? Her friends agreed by the hundreds. In the end, after our baby was born and remained unnamed for three days, Wolfie's father, Norbert, told me to give in, telling me 'Tine was a sweet old grandmother—why not let her have her way? So we named our son Robert Brooks Schaum, a fine old family name. My grandmother wrote a triumphant column letting her readers know that since she'd won the war over his legal name, she'd forego the battle of deciding what we called him among ourselves. She made a mistake, though, in her humble victory statement— she wrote that she was happy with the name and that the new baby's parents might still call him Wolfie.

From time to time, I'd get into this phase where I'd ask her *please* not to write about me at all. She skirted that issue and instead of "Tib" or "my granddaughter Sibley," I'd end up being "a young woman" she knew. That way, she could get in her opinion about, for example, me expecting my husband to get me out of bed and how no one should be responsible for waking anyone else up. Furthermore, Muv let *her* miss school once when 'Tine wouldn't get up after a single motherly shake. And it only took once. She wasn't *staying home*, she was *missing* school.

That was how *Muv* felt about it, how she *herself* felt about it, it was a moral issue of the highest order—it was probably how *God* felt about it. In her column she mercilessly lectured that poor, pathetic young woman she knew. Like I said, it's a strange territory.

That particular instance was tame, however. Another time, years later, she brought her newspaper editor to my house. I won't say what it was in reference to, but I will say, I asked her pointedly not to write about the issue at hand—and I did so in front of her editor so there could be no mistake about my private life ending up on everyone's breakfast table. I looked over her shoulder to her editor standing behind her and said, "You're a witness and you can't let her write that."

"What makes you think *she* can tell me what to do?" my grandmother snapped.

But 'Tine couldn't help herself. I'd seen the column coming over her like a fever. There was no stopping it. Like always, though we talked off and on all day, every day, if I didn't read the paper, I only knew what she wrote from the phone calls I got.

Her next column involved a "young couple looking for a house." This was exactly the situation I asked her not to write about, and I was livid. I called her and told her a grandmother wasn't supposed to do things like that, especially after I'd made such a point of asking her not to. It was one of the worst confrontations we ever had. At the end of the conversation, we were both in tears. I was angry and she was hurt.

Of course, the next day when I woke up, the birds were singing and the sun was shining and I was purged. It took me several tries to get her for our morning call and I doubt she would have answered at all except that I let the phone ring about twenty minutes nonstop. It was childish. But I knew she was sitting right there by the telephone, feeling sorry for herself. I knew how bad her coffee would taste until I said I was sorry.

When she finally picked up, I thought I'd called a house where a funeral was going on. The guilt was overwhelming. It went on for two days, a record. It went on long enough to make a serious impression. I was so distraught over the heartache I had caused my fragile granny, that I *almost* never spoke to her that way again.

✺ I love National Public Radio and keep it on all day while I'm working. I was at my computer typing away when I heard the NPR disc jockey announce how sorry they all were that Celestine Sibley had had a heart attack.

Angered at hearing the announcement on the air, I called the station, asked for the chatty DJ, and said to him, "This is Sibley Fleming. I'm Celestine Sibley's granddaughter and I don't appreciate learning from the radio that my grandmother had a heart attack."

"But it was in her column this morning!" he said apologetically.

I'm sure I blushed, but then I got angry. It wasn't really a heart attack. Or if it was it was a small one. She had been on the phone with me when it happened and she said the bed was shaking, she thought there was a small earthquake. She was sensitive about her health and was reluctant to let even people in the family know what was going on with her. So, after I got finished being put out with the radio, I got put out with her. It wasn't right. What she'd done was dispel nasty health rumors that might have been escalating by telling some part of the truth in her column. That's what she did. Needless to say, I was sorry and got a fast turnaround on my comeuppance.

When I was her assistant, Don O'Briant, the beloved book page editor of the *AJC* who has set Atlanta literary standards for many years, let me write a couple of reviews. When I tried to go any further in the newsroom, cries of nepotism dampened my ideas of writing for the paper. It wasn't a matter of if I *could* write or if I *needed* a job and it likely wasn't even nepotism when I think about it—plenty of families manage to work together at the paper—it just might have been that her colleagues had a hard time viewing me as anything more than grandmother's column fodder. I skirted the issue with an editor who was willing to give me a shot writing under a pen name. Because of the Southern ring to it, I choose Millicent Tate. I wrote an essay and turned it in to my buddy. He was putting his job on the line turning it in for copyediting and print. When his boss wanted to know who this Millicent Tate character was, my friend collapsed under the pressure and told them the truth—*Sibley.*

The powers that were said they wouldn't keep a good writer out of the paper just because of *who* they were related to. As a result, I got to know the feeling of seeing my byline in print for the first time, something akin to magic. You can't believe you see your own name—right there, in print, as good as or better than seeing it on a billboard. The newspaper gets worn out with your fond gazing and from your falling asleep with it clutched to your fast-beating breast. Anybody who tells you different is damn liar.

Not long after that first byline, my grandmother got into a car accident that bruised her up and broke some ribs. I'd been chatting around with an editor at the paper, not with any purpose in mind. I'd off-handedly said something to the editor about how cold my grandmother's cabin was in the winter and comparing Sweet Apple to the chilly old house that I occupied. I got a call from a senior *AJC* editor asking if I could put my thoughts into a column and, if I could, assuring me that the paper would run it while my grandmother was at home recovering.

It's a mistake to think even a grandmother would want to see a granddaughter in her personal column space. When I asked 'Tine what she thought about me writing a column in her absence, if it'd be okay, she said quite seriously, "Ralph McGill never let anyone sub his column." I never did it again, but it was fun, just to see what the format was, if I could do it.

Later I started providing a weekly column for a handful of small papers around the state. I was told to write whatever was on my mind—of course, I drew on my life with my family. My grandmother, as far I know, seldom read these gems of wisdom except one time when one of her loyal readers clipped something I wrote about her and sent it to her. Her response sounded as if she'd just tasted something sour. She said, "You make me sound like a sweet little old lady."

"That's the way I see you," I defended myself. "You're my grandmother."

"Well, I've been writing about you all these years," she conceded, "I guess turnabout is fair play."

Following is the column that she received, sometime after it ran in the *AJC* in July of 1995. It remains one of my favorites.

My phone rang at 9:30 A.M. It was my grandmother. "Go back to sleep—I woke you," she said.

"No you didn't," I said quickly. I really was awake. Nine-thirty to me on some days is more like late afternoon. "I'm up."

"No, you're not. Go back to sleep," she insisted.

I could guess something was up because this also happened to be the day that I was leaving town for a week. "You coming out to visit before you go?" She had "mad money" for me and besides, she said, she would miss me.

Well, I hadn't washed clothes, packed, fed the boys breakfast or checked on the weather report. But one doesn't say "no" to a grandmother because grandmothers are special.

If, for instance, your grandmother wants you to drive 40 miles just to sit in her yard for a cup of coffee when you're trying to get out of town, you do it.

If, when you get to your grandmother's house in the country and she wants to walk over her yard to find the best spot to plant a dish of wild irises somebody gave her and you end up picking blueberries instead, that's okay.

It's your grandmother and just because you're grown doesn't mean that she didn't come prepared for you to pick blueberries. She has a plastic newspaper wrapper tucked into her apron that will hold whatever you find.

After picking blueberries, your grandmother may notice that the blackberries are not all red as she'd thought before. She may suddenly realize if she pulls down a branch from the top of a thicket made up of honeysuckle vines and blue-berry and blackberry bushes, there's a whole swatch of blueberries you missed. And they're ripe.

But that's okay. You pick the soft, sweet berries gingerly because you love your grandmother and it gives you a warm feeling inside to think that you are gathering fruit that will end up on your grandmother's breakfast table.

When the plastic bag is full, you are not surprised, however, when your grandmother hands you the bag of berries and says, "They're to eat on the plane."

You look at your watch. You wonder about that plane and when it might be taking off. If it will take off without you. You notice that your grandmother has now given your youngest child a basket and directed him to collect windfall apples for a pie.

This will take some time. The problem with windfall apples is that they have brown spots and worms but, since they are on the ground, they are the ones that your youngest can reach. There is then a sorting and debating that goes on for 15 minutes.

Your youngest child will want to wash the windfall apples when he's drinking a Coke that your grandmother has given him and, because she thinks washing things in general is a good idea, you go along with the plan.

Having seen the apple project is moving along, your grandmother may remember the double-fudge chocolate cake on her chopping block and decide you look like you need a piece. With a cup of coffee. In the yard.

She may think it's time to take a break on the brick patio while you eat and she convinces you to take the "mad money" for the trip.

If your grandmother speaks, she may tell you how nice it would be for you to spend a week with her playing in the greenhouse, reading, and swinging on the porch. And because it's your grandmother, you will seriously consider changing your plans.

❧ So what? It was a sweet little old lady column. It wasn't really how I felt about every aspect of her—just the way she'd been that day. I also have fond memories of my grandmother's editor coming in with changes from the copy desk. The way the fluorescent light touched her gray curls as she gracefully enveloped the frame of her office door. And if I listen closely, as if to a seashell, I can recall the hum buzz of the printers churning out copy as my grandmother scanned the newsroom with squinted hawk's eyes, and demanded, "Where is the son of a bitch?"

❧ 'Tine latched onto people, became their champion and best friend, sensing something in their character unconsciously, and then holding fast and loyally to the relationship. Ellen Howle was one such person. First, she became my grandmother's assistant, then my roommate, and has graduated over the years to lifetime friend.

In November of 1991, Ellen got a job clerking for the features department at the *Atlanta Journal-Constitution*. She told me later she knew who Celestine Sibley was because her father, Paul Howle, had worked for the *Journal* before the merging of the two daily papers and he had talked about 'Tine being the best reporter in the newsroom. One day Ellen was coming out of the elevator as my grandmother was going towards it.

llen spoke up, "Miss Sibley, I'm Ellen Howle—Paul Howle's daughter, and I've been clerking here on the features floor taking your messages and delivering your mail."

"And you're doing such a fine job, child!" my grandmother said with a warm hand on Ellen's shoulder. "Well, I'm off to Kiwanis for lunch."

Suddenly Ellen blurted out like a little girl, "It's my birthday!"

My grandmother turned, the smile still in place, and said, "Come with me."

Ellen followed 'Tine self-consciously through the corridor of desks that make up the newsroom back to her glass-paned office. There were hundreds of books in piles, on the floor, falling off the desk, papers were everywhere, curled photos salt-and-peppered the room.

"Those are photographs of Clarke Gable," Ellen said in awe.

"Oh, you can have 'em honey," came the crackled, off-hand reply.

Being a good Southern girl, Ellen knew better than to admire anything too enthusiastically and she quickly picked up the photos and put them on top of a pile of papers on my grandmother's desk.

'Tine motioned for her to sit down and pulled a copy of her book *Turned Funny* out of a box on the floor. Ellen was still gawking at other photos of Eleanor Roosevelt and an old witch in an army jacket and sailor's cap that was a figure of Mayhayley Lancaster, the famed psychic of the John Wallace murder trial in Coweta County, Georgia. (My grandmother had covered for the *Constitution* the 1948 murder case in which land tycoon John Wallace was accused of killing share-cropper William Turner in front of eight witnesses. It was proved that Wallace first dumped the body in a well and later retrieved and burned it under cover of night and dumped the ashes in a stream across the Meriwether County line. Sheriff Lamar Potts pursued the case until justice was served. Lancaster's visions of Wallace's movements were revealed to be quite accurate.)

Ellen has since recalled fondly that she shouldn't have worried because 'Tine was busy scribbling something in the front of the book, which she closed and handed back to her.

"Child, books are for sharing," 'Tine said and left for her lunch.

Still sitting in the chair, Ellen opened the book to see the inscription. It read, "To Paula, The brightest and most beautiful addition to our staff in many a long day—Happy Birthday!"

Horrified and speechless, Ellen snapped the book shut and went back to work, wondering how she could politely tell my grandmother her real name. Three days later, Ellen went to see my grandmother in her office.

"I don't mean to interrupt you," Ellen said, clearing her throat as she held out the gift copy of *Turned Funny* and said, "Miss Sibley, I sure enjoyed reading your book and I don't know how to tell you this, but my name is not Paula—"

She didn't bat an eye. "Well, child, what *is* your name? Your father's name is Paul, so shouldn't your name be *Paula?*"

Ellen shook her sassy head.

"Hand me that book," 'Tine said with an outstretched hand. With a pen, she crossed out *Paula*, wrote "I meant Ellen," and clapped the book shut. "All better now."

A week later, Ellen was under my grandmother's employment. And not many more weeks later, my grandmother engaged Ellen as my roommate—a *mole*, if you will. Of course Ellen wasn't that cagy—how could she have known it was an easy way for my grandmother to keep tabs on me and the boys? Ellen Howle was typical of the many young people who crossed my grandmother's path. She was as bad an assistant as I was and later went on to bigger and better things.

One morning, I got a call from 'Tine's office. It was Ellen and she was sobbing. "What's wrong?" I demanded.

"My boyfriend just broke up with me and I don't want your grandmother to see me crying," she sniffled.

I thought about it, the image of my grandmother seeing someone crying over, of all things, a boyfriend, and I said, "She'd probably spit on you. Come to think of it, I'd probably spit on you, too."

Not what Ellen expected to hear. But she knew what I didn't, there is newsroom protocol, standards not to be broken. Reporters have ideals just about as sacred as those of priests. Reporters are seasoned, tough, savvy, and, at all costs, keep their cool. So when I told Ellen that she was gonna get spit on by at least one member of our family, she broke out laughing.

I found out much later that after Ellen had hung up the phone, the tears and loss had hit her again. My grandmother walked in her office and discovered the weeping, frail sight of a girl with a broken heart. 'Tine's reporter instinct kicked in and, as if to protect Ellen from herself, she slapped her across the face—and hard.

"Don't ever cry in the newsroom," 'Tine admonished her.

I guess at that point, being slapped probably was more acceptable to Ellen than being spat on. She immediately dried her eyes and set back to work.

"Now go get us a goodie from the Jesus Lady," my grandmother told her as if nothing out of the ordinary has passed between them.

The Jesus Lady is still there. She's a very pious woman who runs a bakery called Our Heavenly Father & Jesus Bakery next to the newspaper offices and she doesn't bake her cakes with anything that will spoil. She would take one look at Ellen's short work skirt and say, "Young lady, raise your standard, lower your skirt." My grandmother once wrote a column about "a skirt that barely cleared (a young woman's) fanny," but omitted the name of the guilty party.

Anyway, the Jesus Lady never told my grandmother what to do—she was a big fan of 'Tine's. My grandmother tolerated her and her self-righteous ways only because of her delicious cakes. 'Tine didn't approve of people who preached at her. Once, years before, while I was her assistant, someone sent a letter telling her that "Jesus loves you, Celestine Sibley."

"Isn't that nice?" I'd asked with some trepidation. "Should I write a thank-you?"

"No," she said with venom. "Imagine that, someone thinking they can speak for Jesus!"

Another reader who wrote quite frequently was the Armageddon Lady. Not only did she write letters warning us about the fast-coming end of the world, but she sent cakes and crystallized pecans which we all ate hoping the food wasn't laced with cyanide. My grandmother would fish a letter opener out of a desk drawer to take a slice, ceremoniously and mysteriously saying, "I hope it's okay . . ."

✿ The best assistant my grandmother ever had (and maybe the only efficient one) was a lovely woman named Debra Childers. Debra was and is a gentlewoman who 'Tine introduced as being "raised gently." A childhood friend of Debra's once told me that the harshest thing she'd ever heard Debra say was "bummer." There is a compassion about her and an ability to give that is quite rare.

For the last years of my grandmother's life at the newspaper, it was Debra Childers who dealt with letters, phone calls, scheduling, and in no small part, my grandmother's vast and inquisitive family. In the process of my grandmother's work relationship with Debra, 'Tine and I got to know and love her and her husband Richard outside the office, sharing meals, trials, and triumphs.

'Tine and her dog Kazan outside Sweet Apple. She is in her typical at-home garb, something comfy with lots of room.
(Joey Ivansco, *Atlanta Journal-Constitution*)

This photo from the sixties shows what Sweet Apple looked like when 'Tine first moved in. (ATLANTA JOURNAL-CONSTITUTION)

My mother Mary and me at Sweet Apple in 1965 or 1966.

My big brother, Charles Beresford "Bird" Fleming, in front of the apple tree at Sweet Apple in 1971. I called the dress 'Tine made for me my "numbers dress." We'd geared up with basket and tote to go collecting in the woods. (CELESTINE SIBLEY)

Me at about age ten sitting at Georgia Governor George Busbee's desk. Gov. Busbee wanted to have his picture taken with me, but 'Tine wouldn't let him.

My grandmother's house on Dog Island, Florida, was built mostly by family members in the late-1970s. (BILL HENDRICK, ATLANTA JOURNAL-CONSTITUTION)

Playing the flute outside the Roofless Church in New Harmony, Indiana, at about age fifteen. My brother Bird took pictures of everything while working for the school newspaper. (CHARLES FLEMING)

Wolfie (Robert Brooks) Schaum and me a couple of weeks after 'Tine helped bring him into the world and named him. Wolfie's father took this picture and painted a water-color from it which 'Tine displayed in her guest room at Sweet Apple.
(NORBERT SCHAUM)

Jack's Lake was named after my grandmother's second hus-band, Jack Strong, who excavated it. It was close by Sweet Apple and was where we all learned to fish and swim.
(CHARLES FLEMING)

Murder mystery writer Kathy Hogan Trocheck, 'Tine, and me at a party for Anne River Siddons given by her publisher. 'Tine was long a mentor for her friend Kathy.
(Lawrence P. Ashmead)

'Tine at Sweet Apple. This is the place in front of her living room fireplace where she read her morning meditations and said her prayers.
(PRO Studio, McDonough)

This photo of my grandmother and me in her office at the Atlanta Journal-Constitution *was taken in 1997 for use as the author photo for* The Celestine Sibley Sampler. *It was taken quickly—in about two minutes—just about our length of patience for picture-taking.*
(JOEY IVANSCO)

My grandmother would get on anything that would give a fast ride. This was one of her last escapades, riding a Harley-Davidson with then-AJC photo editor Akili Ramsess in the summer of 1999. She wrote in her column afterward that "a woman who rides a motorcycle is in tune with the universe."
(PHIL SKINNER, *ATLANTA JOURNAL-CONSTITUTION*)

'Tine's longtime friend Reverend Patricia Templeton being interviewed after my grandmother's memorial service. Many in the Atlanta media attended the service, both to cover it and as mourners.
(RODNEY HO)

TO SIBLEY - 'TINE WILL BE MISSED.
MIKE LUCKOVICH 9/99

WAIT 'TIL CELESTINE SEES THE CABIN WE BUILT FOR HER...

Cartoon by Mike Luckovich,
Pulitzer Prize-winning cartoonist for the AJC.

CHAPTER FIVE

I was twenty-five years old when I discovered I was pregnant with my second child. True to form, my grandmother was thrilled—there would be no regrets, only celebration for the coming addition to our family. My feelings were mixed. I had already jumped from childhood to parenthood with no break in between. Vincent was just getting old enough to be manageable—out of diapers, sleeping through the night. So I spent the first six or more months of my pregnancy ignoring it.

At a gargantuan eight months, I sat at my grandmother's house, rocking in her living room, while she and her neighbor, Nan, commented on my condition.

"When I was eight months pregnant, I had little baby dresses made, and blankets edged and the baby's room painted," my grandmother told her friend, motioning towards me. "Then look at this child, she hasn't done the first thing . . ."

Nan agreed. She too had provided and readied for all four of her children.

I was rocking and thinking to myself how I didn't see any men edging blankets or buying booties. "I would be getting ready," I said, "but I'm still kicking myself that I got pregnant in the first place."

That was my way of being smart. I had harbored a resentment towards society since my first days in college when I heard the phrase "M.R.S. degree." All of a sudden, after all of my practicing and working and studying, I got to college only to be viewed as a second-class citizen by virtue of my sex.

But I wasn't really kicking myself about the coming baby. Secretly, I was excited about the person who grew inside—each turn, each punch and flutter. Being the only girl among so many boys, I had picked up this very nonchalant cool attitude that I just couldn't shake.

✂ In our family, most periods can be marked by work projects. The big project during Wolfie's gestation was the cabin at Holly Creek. It was 1990 and there was renewed interest in the old cabin where me and my brother had gone as children. 'Tine had bought it for five hundred dollars back when her children were small and they had spent countless weekends hauling rocks to make walls, hanging curtains, fixing up.

Jack had died a few months before in November of 1989 and though my grandmother was being stoic and going on with her life, she was also grieving. So she had an interest in this project that would fill her weekends with memories, smells, and sounds. She'd written her first book, *Malignant Heart*, sitting in the shallow creek with a typewriter balanced on her lap, and over the years the cabin had claimed a hold on each member of our family.

The mountain house was originally a hunter's lodge, I think. It was not posh by any standard. There was no electricity. We got our water in plastic jugs from a spring that ran out of the side of the mountain down the road. The outhouse had long been taken away by storms, as had the back bedroom and a part of the roof. John and Bird were probably responsible for saving the cabin up until the point when we all got interested. My grandmother bought new tin and John, Bird, and Norbert put a roof on the cabin. She bought windows and lumber and the boys fell to and reconstructed the back bedroom. (Previously, there had been a white slop bucket that functioned for those persons too modest to squat in the woods.) I found an ugly wood stove that would serve for heat.

My grandmother packed picnics for our workers and we ate on the porch or by the creek, dreaming up furniture, plants, and the grand possibility of adding electricity should a windfall come.

One Friday, I, though obviously with child but still a functioning size, took Vincent to Holly Creek for a spend-the-night. We loaded up my VW Beetle and arrived at the cabin after nightfall. It was hard to see in the dark, hard to know what was lurking in the cobwebs, under the floorboards broken up with holes. We unloaded our bedding (back then, it wasn't sleeping bags, it was blankets, quilts, and pillows). Finally, situated the best we could manage, we turned off the kerosene lantern and attempted to go to sleep.

We both began to notice a squeaking noise that we couldn't pass off on the rustling of the trees. "What's that?" Vincent asked, sitting bolt upright.

"I didn't hear anything," I lied.

"There's something out there, Mom," my five-year-old whispered nervously, poking my ribs. I sat up, listened, then lay back down.

"Nothing," I said no sooner than I saw two monstrous yellow eyes staring at us from up in the rafters.

In no time flat, we'd packed up the car, driven over the creek and made the two-hour journey back to my grandmother's where we went straight upstairs to the children's room without waking her, and fell fast asleep.

The next morning, she and Vincent were already up when I made my way downstairs. "I asked Vincent why y'all came back," she informed me, "and he said, 'Oh, my Mom got *scared.*'"

⚘ The last day of March in 1990, I had gone to spend the night with my grandmother. Vincent was already at Dog Island with Mom and her brood and had been there for over a week. Norbert was in his cabinetmaking and sculpting workshop working on a hard deadline. 'Tine had fixed up the children's room on "the other side of the house" (that's what we call the second cabin, upstairs) as a place to watch videos, which she had decided were a good and wondrous thing since the technology meant she could re-see her favorite old movies. She dubbed this room "The Roxy" for the old theatre that had been in downtown Atlanta. We rented Jeanette McDonald and Nelson Eddy in the one where they sing "Ah! Sweet Mystery of Life."

My cousin Ted was staying with her but he had no interest in old black-and-white romances so 'Tine and I fixed ourselves dinner, popped popcorn, and watched our movie without his company.

I was already ten months pregnant, my second child as late as the first. Everyone had tired of waiting for me to go into labor suspecting, as I did, that the child was forthcoming no time soon. Me and 'Tine were going to get barbecued chicken and invite any remaining family members we could find to the cabin for a Sunday supper. While Jeannette and Nelson sang, I began to feel some uncomfortable goings-on in my middle, each grunt pricking up my grandmother's ears with curious delight. But, of course, no baby was coming. And it was time for bed. I said I'd sleep in the children's room and not bother 'Tine with my tossing and turning since I hadn't been sleeping well for weeks.

"Aw shoot," she scoffed, "you can't wake me up. Besides, I'd feel better to have you by my side so I can keep an eye and birth a baby if I need to."

I wasn't going to argue. I liked sleeping in her bed—I imagine we all did. If you slept on the other side of the house, she was sure to get up a few times in the middle of the night to check on you anyway. I put on some pajamas and climbed in with her.

The next morning, she was up early and had coffee brewing and the smell of toast, bacon, and grits wafting from the kitchen. I waddled in and nursed a cup of coffee.

"There is no baby," I said feebly and forlorn. "It's never coming. I'm going to look like this forever—you just wait and see."

'Tine had nothing to say to this. She was trying to decide if she should go to church or not—she'd already fished out a wool skirt and panty hose from her closet and put them on. She smelled, as usual, like Old English lavender soap and mothballs. Ted joined us in the kitchen with a basketball and announced that he was going to find a game.

"Will you be alright by yourself until I get back, honey?" 'Tine asked casually. But I know now she had other ideas.

Being a surly twenty-something, I am sure I said something slightly sarcastic with a tinge of self-pity. My grandmother disappeared upstairs to her bedroom and came back down in jeans and a sweatshirt. "I believe I'll skip church today and we can take a walk down the road together," she told me cheerfully.

I loved walking with my grandmother, especially at Sweet Apple. I would not be put off by those extra forty-five pounds or the way I huffed and puffed or the way I had to go to the bathroom every ten seconds. I was going to a walk down the road with "Tine.

There may have been a little extra bounce in her step— looking back, I believe there was. We started for a short stroll down the road and every time we'd hit a bend, she'd say, "Just a little bit further." She could have been a professional athlete if she'd wanted to, she had that kind of endurance, well into her eighties even. As we walked she told me how Muv had taken her for a long walk once and it had induced labor.

"Fat chance," I thought to myself, and then she was bounding off the road into the woods and down a hill. I followed with no small amount of difficulty. She kept seeing a flower or a tree or a dump or a rock or the wispy tail of a deer in the distance. And she kept going for the distance like she was trying to climb over the horizon—with me trailing behind.

When we got back to her yard—I swear this is the truth although she told it differently, that I was begging to go to the hospital and she was as cool as a cucumber—that funny jerking-in-the-middle feeling was getting me again.

"What was that?" she asked as I sat in the swing clutching my stomach.

"Nothing," I defended myself. And then that nothing happened again and then again.

"Let me take you to town to the hospital," she offered. "I think you're going into labor."

"No. I don't want to go all the way to town and find out it was false labor and then we'll miss our supper and no barbecued chicken. It's not labor," I assured her.

She was hopping about and was as energetic and beside herself as if she were in the midst of breaking news and she had the scoop. She called the hospital and they described something to her, some indication about when it was time to go.

"We're going to town," she said with finality.

"I'm gonna feel stupid. I doubt it's labor. Don't make me go to town—it'll waste the whole day," I complained with a yawn. But I was jerked to alertness by a sudden pain. I really didn't know what the beginning of natural labor felt like because I hadn't gone through it with Vincent in Ireland. He'd been so late, they made labor happen medically.

She didn't take any more lip—she got me in the car, reminding me that she didn't want to have to bring that baby into the world herself. She gave me her watch to hold in the car and boy, the pains were deep and getting closer and closer together.

We were just on the highway when she asked, "What's the name gonna be?"

"Wolfgang," I said through clenched teeth.

"Robert Brooks," she corrected me.

"No, 'Tine. It's gonna be Wolfgang—the baby *will be* half German—"

"I am going to pull this car over to the side of the road and put you out on the highway if you name that child *Wolfgang*. It sounds like a wolf or something. How about a fine old family name like Robert Brooks?"

It was not responsible of me to disagree because she could have put me out by the side of the road but I stood my ground and did not give in. Standing your ground with my grandmother was something like standing your ground against a world leader or a seasoned politician—they all are capable of wearing you down. They have that kind of patience, the kind that can wait until they get their way or forever, whichever comes first.

We stopped by my house to pick up Norbert. When we got to Crawford Long Memorial Hospital, where I had been born and where Ted and many other babies in our family had been born, there was precious little time to do anything but push. I was screaming because it hurt really badly and apparently I was making nervous other patients who thought I was dying in my birthing room. My grandmother sat in the hall with a lady who had a bucket of fried chicken. The woman noted the screaming and said, "Listen to all that carrying on. I wonder who *that one* belongs to?"

My grandmother held up a greasy finger indicating that she was the owner of the screamer.

🐝 The baby came into the world in fifteen minutes flat. Born April 1, 1990, April Fool's Day, and, incidentally, twenty-four hours after the insurance had lapsed. Norbert and I brought our son home unnamed and he remained in his little nameless state for three days while me and my grandmother haggled. She came to town to dicker over his cradle and she was equally comfortable exponding on her point over the phone. Finally Norbert gave in and shamed me, telling me it was a small thing to do for a grandmother who meant so much. The birth certificate was filled out "Robert Brooks"—Robert after Pap, and Brooks from my grandfather's fine Mobile side of the family.

'Tine, as I mentioned, wrote a piece about the naming of Wolfie and, although she was probably just filling in the last bit of space she needed in her column if she wasn't being outright humble about her victory, she wrote that we might still call him Wolfie. And, of course, that's just what we have done.

❧ As a wise man once said, there are no innocent victims in the marital graveyard. So when I woke up one day and said to myself, "I can call it six years or I can call it sixteen," I knew that the end had arrived. Once I'd made up my mind, I got a job, a lawyer, and an apartment. It sounds brutal and it was— Vincent was only five and Wolfie was fresh in the world, just a few months old.

When 'Tine found out, she worried. How was I going to take care of myself and the boys? Wouldn't it be better to change my mind or to wait and think it over? In response to my bad decision, there was no help on the way from anyone related to me by blood. If I was going to break up a family, I'd have to do it alone. And I did. My grandmother had gone to Italy to visit Walter and Larry. When she returned, my life, at least on the surface, had changed overnight.

That first year was one of the hardest I've ever been through. It was also one of the most liberating. From then on, I knew, I was responsible for my own happiness and if I didn't succeed I had no one to blame but myself. I still don't know how I did it or how anyone else does.

Every morning I got up at 5:00 A.M., changed the baby's diaper, dressed both children, drove them across town to a child-care place and showed up at work at Peachtree Publishers by 7:30. I seldom took lunch and I always took work home for fear that my employer would think I wasn't capable of handling the load. At night after I picked up the children and did some shopping or whatever errands I needed to run, I bathed the boys, fed them, read to them (without fail), and put them in bed—Wolfie had to be rocked the requisite hour since he was so small. Then, as if my day hadn't been long enough, I would do some of the work I'd brought home and then write on my own creative stuff until I fell asleep. Each day was a repeat. I was afraid to stop working and doing in the event that the house of cards I had built would all fall apart.

It took a while for my grandmother to come around. The idea of leaving a husband who had a job and who, though we didn't get along, loved me, was foreign to her.

✁ A year or so later, in 1992, Ellen Howle started working for 'Tine and she began rooming with Vincent, Wolfie, and me. Ellen was my grandmother's direct information pipeline from our house to her office. 'Tine liked to keep track of me and the boys as if she were keeping track of horses she'd bet her life savings on. And, in a way, since we were part of her family, she had.

The boys loved Ellen who was gentle, funny, and who liked to cook. The only drawback to our union was that living together was like having an eternal pajama party. Ellen and I stayed up late and giggled, rehashed old crushes, sighed over new crushes, and plotted world domination. We were both broke—me at a subsistence level with taking care of the boys, and her clerking part-time at the newspaper.

One weekend when the boys had gone to their dad's and Ellen had gone to her parents, my grandmother came to spend the night. It was cool weather—chilly in the morning with just enough sun in the afternoon to warm things up before the evening frost came.

The gas had been cut off for non-payment and we didn't have the thousand dollars it would take to turn it back on. Instead, me and Ellen had been inventive. We heated the boy's bath water in the microwave and told them they were taking Indian baths. We plugged in useless electric heaters, employed old electric blankets, and nuked everything from oatmeal to toast in the microwave.

My grandmother arrived early in the day. She and I had house projects planned—painting over rotten wood, planting flower boxes, and hiding unsightly holes in the plaster with pictures and furniture. She mentioned the house was a bit nippy and asked if I would turn on the heat.

"I'm trying to save money while the boys are away," I told her. "I'll get you a sweater."

Well, the sweater was fine for a while. The day drew on and the sun poured through the windows warming what spaces it reached. But 'Tine was still cold. I offered her an electric heater for her toes.

Electric heaters are good for bathrooms and spot heating but don't allow for comfortable roaming around a big old house with a bowling alley hallway and ten-foot ceilings.

"Sibley, I'm *cold*. Turn on the heat," 'Tine demanded.

"I don't think I can," I said, fishing for a way to avoid telling the truth. "It's not working at the moment."

"What do you mean it's not working? How long has it been broken?"

"The problem is that place where the gas goes into it. Well, there's no gas going into it," I offered vaguely.

She stood a moment trying to decipher, then a light flashed on over her head. "Did you pay the bill?"

I tried to skirt the issue. My pride couldn't take admitting that I'd let the gas go off, but then there was no way to heat that house, no way at all. There were pieces of flooring miss-ing and the glass in the windows hung by sheer balance rather than by putty. What we finally came up with was an old-fashioned heating system. Out by the goat shed at Sweet Apple, standing in the rain, there was an old wood stove that had once been in Jack's house. 'Tine insisted we haul it to town and set it up in the dining room.

You would think a wood stove wouldn't have much chance of working in a city environment but we always had plenty to burn. We gathered the kindling from the yard, fallen branches and twigs. Too, if we drove around after a storm, we were sure to find stumps, whole blocks of fuel discarded on the side of the road. When we gutted a room, we tossed in the old wood slats from behind the plaster—we were recycling and we were warm.

When 'Tine came to visit ever after and the weather was cool, Ellen and I prepared a rocking chair, laid a fire, and offered a woolen lap blanket. In these conditions, she was just as happy (perhaps more so) as if we'd had insulation and cen-tral heat. Now, I'll just say this. The smell of fresh cut oak logs is dank and edgy to the nose. But 'Tine loved that smell almost as much as some people love the smell of money or as much as she loved the smell of the truckload of chicken manure that she got every spring.

Later, after Ellen had moved on to more comfortable accommodations, we had another set of roommates, also compliments of 'Tine. Somehow, perhaps through 'Tine's church, she and my mother had met a Russian mother and daughter and they ended up staying with us a couple of months. Natasha, the mother, had been a scientist in Moscow. Her daughter, Maya, was about ten years old, pale white, and thin. Her blond hair was about as light as her skin, and I guess for that reason, I always thought of her as a sort of snowbird.

"How's your handmaiden?" 'Tine would ask as if she'd bequeathed me household help.

Getting waited on wasn't quite the way it went. Natasha got jobs and I added Maya to my list of children to pick up from school and worry about. I wasn't in the position to accept housework in lieu of rent.

Christmas came and it was time to get a tree. Natasha couldn't fathom the wastefulness of buying a tree when there were so many in the park. She told me that her Maya didn't need a tree, all they had for Christmas in Russia were cranberries which they gathered in the woods outside of the city and kept cold on the windowsill.

I insisted, and took the children to a tree lot. When the tree was bedecked with ornaments and the lights plugged in, Maya, inhaling deep with excitement, said in strained English, "But Sib-lee, it eez beau-tee-ful!" I felt like such a grand and magnanimous human being, so giving, such a hero.

The irony of all this was that that very night Natasha informed me that she and Maya were going for a two-week ski vacation in Colorado with some friends—that was what they'd been saving their money for.

I told my grandmother early the next morning on the phone. "Imagine that," she whispered.

❧ From the point that I became a single mother until the day my grandmother died, our lives were virtually inseparable. I was single and alone and so was she.

I think some family members saw our relationship as me being her "project" and her being my benefactress—but nothing could have been further from the truth. We helped each other get along both spiritually and pragmatically.

She stood by and watched as I made mistakes with the understanding that we each had to make our own. We had arguments, mostly because I was so judgmental. When backed into a corner and exasperated, she'd say, "You know how I know? I was that way when I was young, too."

Her biggest praise was for survival. The ultimate compliment, which 'Tine gave with reverence, was "I believe you're like Muv. You have that kind of strength. Muv would be proud of you."

But being on my own didn't turn out exactly to be the liberating experience I thought. Checks didn't always come when they were supposed to. When I started writing as a freelancer, I learned how to make a tidy sum in a short period of time, but I couldn't quite nail down how to keep new assignments coming in steadily. I was never picky about the kind of work I took on—if it was written and it paid, I'd pen a restaurant menu.

❧ Later, Polly Goolsby came into our lives. She worked twenty hours a week, picking the boys up after school, cleaning, and grocery shopping. My grandmother helped me pay Polly and I helped my grandmother with her paperwork and drove her to signings, dinners, and speaking engagements. We all said we were helping each other out but I do not know how I would have managed without the two of them.

Polly was a miracle worker with the grocery money and could stretch fifty dollars into a week's worth of meals. She didn't mind that the new dryer I bought didn't have the right hook-up—she hung the boys' clothes on a line and when it was raining, over the backs of chairs indoors. 'Tine made regular stops by Goodwill and Salvation Army and bought needed items like towels and sheets and place mats.

'Tine made a set of curtains for me. On the way to the paper one morning, she stopped by my house and we hung them together, opting for nails over the awkward screws that came with the hangers for the curtain rods. We put a curtain over the front door because 'Tine worried that folks could see in when I walked around in my shimmy.

"You go outside and pretend you're a bill collector and I'll hide behind the curtains and pretend I'm not home," she said, opening the door.

Me and the boys liked having my grandmother as spend-the-night company. In a world of uncertainty, it was a comfort, a familiar reminder of family and the greater order of life.

But there was always the preparation. Long ago I had learned that on spend-the-night days, it was best not to assume that I could leave the dishes in the sink. My grandmother would point out that I should have stuck them in a pan and hidden them in the oven if I didn't have time to wash them. Or, failing the oven trick, she'd remind me of the clean white dish cloth method which entails covering dirty dishes with a dish cloth after neatly stacking them on the counter.

The boys would clean their room in anticipation of 'Tine's visit, filling their closet to the bulging point. I would change the sheets on my bed, scrub the bathroom, and tidy up around the front door because grandmothers don't like stumbling over cat dishes and yard toys.

The boys and I would plan special food. We'd want to have something sweet on hand when my grandmother came, maybe donuts dusted with powdered sugar, vanilla wafers, or lemon coolers.

When all was ready, we waited. We'd listen for the sound of her car in the driveway so that we could go out to greet her and carry in her overnight bag which always contained more books than clothes. We looked forward to the bedtime ritual of pajama changing and good-nights in the hall.

So when we got the news one day that my grandmother was coming and bringing my little sister Betsy, we were all abuzz. 'Tine had tickets to *West Side Story* at the Fox Theatre in Atlanta and wanted to take Vincent and my sister Betsy, younger than I by twenty-one years. In honor of company, I baked a ham and made split-pea soup—carefully disposing of the dishes as I went.

'Tine and Betsy arrived and insisted on a pre-theater trip to the Varsity drive-in where, according to my grandmother's friend Larry, everything is fried but the Cokes. The ham steeped in its juices back home as we wolfed down chili dogs and frozen orange drinks instead.

At the Fox, as my grandmother, sister, and eldest son Vincent stepped out of the car, Wolfie and I waved them off and promised to be back by the end of the show.

It is not easy keeping a six-year-old awake until ten o'clock at night. First we made popcorn and watched a video. When that was done, we cut pictures out of the newspaper and lay on the daybed in my office telling stay-awake stories.

As we believed the curtain to be dropping across town, Wolfie and I slogged to the car—he with a blanket and me with a cup of strong coffee.

And let me tell you, like having the right sweets on hand, it is a good feeling to know that you are keeping your grandmother out of the rain by waiting for her in front of a theater.

Except grandmothers aren't predictable. Although the crowd had thinned and the ushers were about to lock up, Wolfie and I still had no passengers to save. As it turned out, an usher told us, "The tall woman with the two small children? I put them in a cab."

❧ I was a workaholic. I worked every possible minute I could grab and if there wasn't work, I'd work on getting work. I was a single mother with no college degree, two children, and a precarious profession.

"I was always so happy if I could get off early from work. I'd rush right home and get a little time with my children," 'Tine told me, trying to get the fact into my head that while work would always be there, children would not.

Since I wouldn't stop work willingly, she would lure me out to the country on the weekends under the guise that she would watch the boys, thus freeing me to work on my laptop. Her real object, however, was to get me and my heathen children to church and out on the open road for long drives through the north Georgia mountains. Her object was to get me to stop and breath in life, to get out of the office which my children had already dubbed "The Dungeon."

'Tine worried about my social life—I had none—and sometimes got tickets to the Altanta Symphony to entice me out of the house. She took interest in my fleeting beaus, the main requirements for her being that they be Presbyterian and Democrat and that they have jobs. Of course my requirement was that they didn't mind dating me, the boys, and 'Tine—no small criterion. So not only was it hard to get me out on a date—the idea of carrying on a relationship with all else in my life held little appeal for me—I had so much baggage I could have opened a small emotional luggage shop.

But there were other ways to get me out. There were spend-the-night trips and house parties with my grandmother's old friends like Bill and Lucy Emerson and Joe and Emily Cumming. They all knew how to have fun and were the poster children for the fact that youth is most definitely wasted on the young. They'd stay up late—long after I had thrown in the towel—exchanging war stories about old working haunts like *Newsweek,* the *Saturday Evening Post,* and the *Atlanta Journal* and the *Atlanta Constitution* before the two papers merged. They didn't have casual conversations, they had *debates.* I was just a grandchild, but these old friends were my grand-mother's contemporaries, her *equals*—and she loved every minute spent with them.

It shows my uneducated sense of humor, but I swear I laughed every time my grandmother told how once she'd asked how Lucy was and Bill had replied, "Fine, if you like Lucy."

✖ I thought of Bill Emerson as a sort of Prince Charming and asked him to write one of the introductions for *The Celestine Sibley Sampler.* He worried about being edited, say-ing he had a very nice story he would give me in exchange for no edit. Of course if I edited, he said, he'd have to take the story back. Doubting someone of Mr. Emerson's stature would need any editing at all, I agreed. The deal being made, he confided, "Sibley, sometimes you have to stoop to con-quer."

Occasionally, as on my thirtieth birthday, instead of a party, 'Tine gave me manuscript revisions to look over. It wasn't that she'd listen to anything I had to offer any more than Bill Emerson would have, but she'd pay me a few dollars and sit still while I gave her my two-cents worth of advice.

In fact 'Tine was so touchy about edits that one time, when her then-editor at the newspaper, Krista Reese, was going on leave to get married, I cornered her replacement and said confidentially, "'Tine likes a *heavy* edit." Krista overheard the wicked remark and immediately set the poor woman straight.

❦ But it was a little like the pot calling the kettle beige, 'Tine telling me I needed to let up on work and have some fun. She was herself a diehard workaholic. She'd work so hard at her job, showing up for events, meeting family obligations, that by fall of every year, she'd end up with a life-threatening case of pneumonia which she would always ignore.

You could not make her stay in her sickbed, not under any circumstances. One time there was a Friends of the DeKalb (County) Library award ceremony in Dunwoody, a northern suburb of Atlanta, where she was going with the Emersons to accept an honor. Beforehand, she stopped by my house after work for a nap and a change of clothes. Her skin burned with fever and a dangerous cough came from deep in her lungs. I tried to stop her from attending the award ceremony. I really tried. The only help she'd accept was my arm as she made her way down the front steps to get into her car.

After about an hour Bill and Lucy Emerson called. Where was my grandmother, they wanted to know. I filled them in. And then began the worry process. Another hour passed and four more phone checks with her hosts at the library and she was nowhere to be seen. We were ready to call all the hospitals when a kindly gentleman called the Emersons. Apparently, too weak to go on, 'Tine had pulled to the side of the road to take a nap. She refused to go to the hospital but she gladly crashed at the Emerson's house.

No one likes the hospital, me included. My mother, being a cautious worrier, believes in trips to the hospital and wasn't beyond calling the occasional ambulance for 'Tine's ills. Another such pneumonia time, Mom told me she was taking 'Tine in.

I had been editing a book about how to tell if your doctor is any good or not. There was a section in the book about how when old people got into the hospital, it was often downhill from there. I dialed the phone and rang until my poor, sick granny answered.

"No matter what happens," I advised her, "don't let them take you to the hospital—" And then I read her the passage of doom. Discovering what I'd done, my mother was, needless to say, quite put out.

✼ So 'Tine and I worried back and forth. Often enough, the morning call would consist of 'Tine trying to figure out if I had enough money. Being from the South, I was raised with the tenet that you did not discuss money, religion, or politics. (Our family had never adhered to the part about politics—that was open season).

"Fine. A gracious plenty! I'm rolling in the dough," I'd lie. Then I'd recount what paychecks I had pending, omitting the larger amounts of outstanding bills. "Don't worry so much," I'd assure her. "If I needed something, I'd tell you."

"You never tell me!" she'd come back with just about the truth. Pride prevented me from admitting that I was short of cash. I always thought it best to *pawn* instead of *borrow.* I got so friendly with the owner of one pawn shop, I signed copies of my book for children to the pawnbroker's kids.

I don't know how much of the time I fooled her—she'd tell me after the fact that she often knew something wasn't right. I hated those checks she pressed in my hand and the money she slipped in my purse. Taking her money made me feel defeated, as if I couldn't manage on my own. 'Tine had other ideas about helping. "You don't have anyone like I did," she'd say. "Muv used to help me out with checks now and then and she'd come and help me with the children when I needed her. Don't be too proud to accept a little help—it's not becoming on my good child."

One Christmas, when our family had gathered at Sweet Apple, after the older boys had opened their gifts of white dress shirts (no thrill for a teenage boy!) and the press releases had been shaken out of all the books, 'Tine grabbed my arm and took me upstairs.

"I want to give you your present here," she said in quiet tones. "I really worked on this one and I want you to have it."

The present was in a small gold box with a ribbon tied on top—one of her ribbons, old and re-ironed after many uses. My fingers shook slightly and I smiled a questioning smile.

Inside was a beautiful gold Hamilton wind-up watch on a black band.

"Muv got it with her first week's pay when she came to Atlanta in the early fifties and worked for an old gentleman as his cook. She wanted me to have a nice watch and she bought it in the middle of the day and came down to the paper to give it to me. Now I want you to have it," she said.

We got it out of the box and slipped it around my wrist under my sweater since it was a secret gift between the two of us. 'Tine didn't want to cause family strife by giving one grandchild something more thoughtful than she had given the others.

"It's so nice," I said with fear. "But what if . . . ?"

"You pawn it if you need to. I did many a time."

CHAPTER SIX

While her driver's license said she was born in 1923, I suspect 'Tine's birthdate was closer to what the newspapers said when she died, about 1914. It's hard to say if anyone could know for certain her exact age anyway—she was born at home and her age was perhaps the best kept secret in her life. Her duplicity was aided by the fact that she consistently lied about it in vast variation long before data was computerized and accurate records could be kept.

I will not attempt to put my grandmother in context with her times but I will say a few things about how the world changed during 'Tine's long life. Fourteen years before she was born, the world's population was 1.65 billion people and a couple of months after she died, the six billionth person was born. Maybe that's why, rapidly, during the course of her life, her big world kept getting smaller and smaller. What was far away became close. What was foreign became commonplace. Even her start in life, the opportunities she had, could never be repeated, for example, her beginning work at a fair-size newspaper at age fifteen, are as gone now as free land.

Phones, cars, planes, computers, short skirts, rock and roll, civil rights, World War II, electricity, helicopters, men on the moon, exploration of Mars, AIDS, eradication of small pox, television. She began life at the end of an era that essentially stretched from the beginning of time and she lived in the century that likely may have done the most to bring about the end of time. Not only did she live in it, she helped to shape it—something she wouldn't readily admit.

✀ There were certain ideas and issues that came up in modern life that Tine couldn't understand. Psychological depression was one of them. She did not believe in depression in terms of anything other than a lack of willpower. Muv had always told her to wash her hair, take a walk, or read a book— that was all that was ever needed to soothe a troubled mind.

For me, depression hit me before I even had a name for it. I remember being very panicked when I was nine years old and the idea of death had become real. I worried about my time on this earth; no, it was as if I meditated on the end to the point of obsession. In my early adulthood, I would have said my depression was really just a melancholy brought on by a rough childhood, unrealized dreams, and unrealistic expectations. It wasn't until later years that a friend described to me his depression and the treatment and how a little medication lifted the horrible haze of misery. Although my depression was only mild, I decided to try this path and the difference it made was worth any inconvenience or fear of what other people might think.

Before the medication, shrinks were an interesting part of my life. As a writer, I enjoyed analyzing what made me tick and the therapy actually did keep the depression at bay. 'Tine was interested in hearing what my shrinks had to say on this or that topic, but beyond the specific conversation, the information fell out of her mind like it was falling off the side of a cliff.

Her attitude towards boredom was venomous. People who got bored were inevitably evil in her book. We called it the *B-word*—people were not allowed to be bored.

Drunks were boring. Of course, 'Tine drank, but only moderately, because, as she always told me, she didn't like the feeling of being out of control. She never smoked cigarettes, except once, over lunch in a boardroom at the paper in an effort to show me what I looked like when I myself smoked. She held the cigarette between her thumb and forefinger like you see in old black-and-white movies. And coughed and coughed.

Knowing our family history, I am not sure how the evils of mental anguish missed her except that perhaps it was her close tie to practicality and the earth that kept her sane. Or maybe she just kept things simple enough to understand. She could equate about any mood with a seasonal change and most of the time, come out of a mood (if a day later) with a favorable spin. But she appreciated other peoples' troubles and was easily drawn to the underdog in most situations.

It wasn't that she was unfeeling or that true feelings couldn't be related to her, it was just that she had never been allowed the leisure of melancholy or the privilege of being bored. Time was a precious commodity and she had a way of processing and accepting life that eliminated the things which she would call "silly," her ultimate insult.

On serious issues, such as suicide, she told me that, as much as she loved life, it was her belief that suicide is a personal choice, just as abortion is. She'd recite the Dorothy Parker poem "Résumé" to lighten the mood:

Razors pain you;
Rivers are damp;
Acids stain you;
And drugs cause cramp.
Guns aren't lawful;
Nooses give;
Gas smells awful;
You might as well live.

She didn't, of course, want to experience suicide or abortion herself or through anyone close to her. It seemed somehow that if there was a choice in such matters, then there was some empowerment, some avenue of prevention. I think she might have been right.

During our long doleful conversations, she sometimes may have been impatient and indifferent, but she always acted as if she were completely interested and took my questions and ideas seriously.

"That may be . . . ," she'd say, seemingly conceding a point when she didn't actually agree, only to casually launch into a damn convincing argument.

On the odd occasion, she'd throw in the towel in an argument but, as the old saying goes "sometimes it's easier to lose than it is to win." The signal of the end of one of these arguments was, "You may be right." It was no victory to see my grandmother give up.

As an example, she thought book acknowledgments were silly. You could see in her eyes the disdain that cut like freshly sharpened razors at the thought. There was a vision of a simpering blond actress gushing about "all of the wonderful people who made it possible."

"Acknowledgments are good," I defended the practice. "It's not for the author."

"It's not?" she stopped suddenly, digesting this foreign thought.

"Think about all those people who work on books and help make them happen but they're not writers so they don't get any credit unless they get thanked—"

Enough said. As long as she wasn't putting on silly airs, as long as it was something for someone else, then it was okay. She made a long list for her next book, a mystery I think, and thanked the world. She may even have enjoyed it.

❦ Her friends didn't like to get in the middle of our little verbal fencing matches and would back off no matter how hard either of us tried to drag them in. On the one hand, if they agreed with her, they were ganging up on her child. On the other, if they agreed with me, they'd be disagreeing with her.

We'd been having a running argument about the Monica Lewinsky/Bill Clinton scandal and the accountability of presidents when we sat down to lunch one day with Tom Downs, her good friend and accountant. We were at Clell's diner in Marietta. There was anticipation of the fresh banana pudding and Clell's wonderful biscuits, meats, and vegetables, none of which worked towards dampening our respective views.

She'd said something about how horrible it was that the press didn't just leave the president alone. She had long been used to politicians keeping mistresses, having casual girlfriends, even using prostitutes.

"He lied under oath!" I nearly yelled. Then, turning to Mr. Downs, I said, "She doesn't care. She thinks it's okay to be a womanizer and to lie—do you?"

"I'm not getting into the middle of this one," Mr. Downs said easily. When I tried to enter my opinion in greater detail, he offered that since she was my grandmother, I might just give in this once. And I did, that once.

❧ Family was another issue entirely. Bill Emerson said it in her eulogy—she was fiercely loyal. And she wanted all of her kinfolk to get along like the characters in *Little Women*. She loved having her children and grandchildren all around her even if half of us weren't speaking to each other, even if our civility was not deeply felt and we were just being well behaved.

During times of family conflict, in order to get everyone around the same table, she'd simply invite us individually and omit the fact to each that she'd asked anyone else. I'm sure like all families we could have been more accepting of each other, more tolerant and forgiving, but certainly I am not the one to speak on that score.

Family grudges are usually born out of minor stupidities and hurt feelings, misplaced jealousy, gossip. The problem is that when they're not dealt with, they escalate and take on the faces of more sinister monsters until no one can remember what they were about in the first place.

On family feuds, my grandmother did not budge. She grew up as an only child and wished that all of her descendants would get along and love each other. She did not appreciate hearing one child dressing down another and, more than once, she chided me for getting my feelings hurt. It started in childhood. When I was growing up, if I came crying that this one or that one had hurt my feelings, she would say, "Oh, for goodness sake. Your feelings can only be hurt if you let them."

This is probably not true. That old sticks-and-stones adage is likely one of the least true things ever repeated in history. One day, Wolfie came to me with his little friend Jabari. They were arguing over the truthfulness of sticks and stones. Wolfie piped up, "It's not true! Is it Mom? It's not. Stick and stones may break your bones but bones will heal. Words can stay with you for the rest of your life."

I like to think that my grandmother had a completely open mind and chose what was right and good nearly all the time. My mother amended this idea for me. "Mother always wanted to have an open mind and to be good. Sometimes it was a struggle," she said. And I might add that open-minded-ness is a struggle for anyone who must exert their will in order for their mind to be opened.

When I worked for 'Tine, I remember her getting a letter from Anita Bryant who had been recently inducted into the downtown Atlanta Kiwanis Club. I couldn't say now what the letter argued, but 'Tine's response in her column is burned into my mind. She was pointed in letting her readers know that she liked homosexuals a whole lot more than she liked Anita Bryant.

But the point is, my grandmother *did* struggle and seek the truth, and in that, I believe she was an example.

❦ My grandmother fell into the category of an accidental public figure. Celebrity was nothing she ever strove for; it just evolved and she took it as part of her job, and maybe, in part, as just being a human, doing public service.

When I started in publishing, it gave our relationship a whole other dimension. She wasn't one to give encourage-ment to a child's face; her idea of child-rearing didn't include producing big heads—*that* was considered unwise.

I remember having lunch with Margaret Quinlin, the president of Peachtree Publishers, on the front porch of my old house in town, the house I shared with Ellen. I'd worked for Peachtree as assistant to the publisher learning the ins and outs of how a publishing house is run a couple of years before I set out freelancing and writing books. Margaret was patiently reading over bits and pieces of story ideas. She'd been supportive of my first essays and columns and offered encouragement. We were talking randomly about possibilities when my grandmother pulled up in the driveway apropos of nothing. She was just in the neighborhood.

"What are you girls up to?" she asked, eyeing Margaret who was also her regional publisher. Margaret told her something about how talented I was and something about how proud she must be.

My grandmother was nonplused. "I don't want to hear how talented she is," 'Tine said, looking over Margaret's shoulder towards me. "She's young. You want to hear things like 'she's coming along,' but I'm getting mail from *my* readers about Sibley."

Later I picked up a carbon of a letter my grandmother had written to Larry and Walter, and my name jumped out. I couldn't help but take a peek at what she'd written: "Sibley continues to be my pride and joy . . ." And I thought I'd been a lot of trouble.

As for book signings, I guess since she was always doing them, they were normal to me. Normal like tourists. Normal like governors and newspapers. At her signings she always had a long line which would snake around the bookstore and, lots of times, right out the door and onto the sidewalk. Her signings were a marvel in and of themselves and legendary to booksellers in the South.

When we were small, Bird and I would get up in front of the signing table and try to get her attention. She might stop for a minute and introduce us to whoever she was signing for. Then we'd go behind the table and sit. I don't remember if we got left with her because Mom had shopping or because 'Tine was actually left babysitting. We must have been a distraction, bored little children, wanting her attention but having to share it with strangers. It was the same as with the parties she gave—grownups, glancing down at us, saying, "Do you know how wonderful your grandmother is?" and we're thinking, or at least I'm thinking, "Of course she's wonderful! Aren't all grandmothers?"

She was known for taking off her shoes while she made a speech. One anecdote that she loved to tell, one she repeated many times when she was at a podium and felt she was getting too much laud and pomp, was one that was based in truth. She'd say, oh sure she was a celebrity, people recognized her all the time.

Every morning she drove to a grocery store near her home, left her car in the parking lot, and took the bus to town. One morning while she was waiting for the bus, she'd noticed her stockings had runs so she dashed to the grocery and bought a new pair. She'd go on with the story and talk about all the things a person could do in the back seat of a car but putting on stockings wasn't one of them. She'd go on and do an impression of herself, between two open car doors quickly scooching up her new stockings before her bus came. And it was at this point that a man walked up—'Tine's behind blowing in the breeze—and said, "Aren't you *Celestine Sibley?*"

❦ 'Tine loved signings for the most part—unless there were too many and then she'd get a grudge that she was *having* to sign when she could be out working in her yard. But, if they were well spaced on her calendar, she really enjoyed them. She liked meeting the people who came to get books signed and was interested in hearing who they were, where they came from, their experiences.

A family member of an author can get *too* used to signings, can look at them as *too* much work and not enough play. Such was the case with me when she was signing at a store called Final Touch in Decatur, Georgia. Final Touch signings are considered in some ways the crème de la crème of Atlanta signings, especially since Atlanta's dear old Oxford Bookstore has closed. At Final Touch, they don't just let any ole author sit behind a table and peddle books. When an author is asked to sign there, the writer has no doubt that they are wanted and all of their friends and readers will be showing up. The store caters these events with wine and wonderful food—the environment is more like a party than a business function. Everyone gets a drink, stands in line with their books, chats, and shops. It's fun.

At a signing at Final Touch for her latest mystery novel, 'Tine was having the time of her life—talking up a storm, drinking white wine, writing whole chapters instead of just *Best wishes.* She kept track of me, peering over the sea of bodies that stood in front of her signing table and calling out to me as in a game of Marco Polo. I had talked to everyone and had eaten everything I cared to. I had shopped around the store, picked out and purchased several books. I was eyeing that snaky endless line wondering if it would ever go down. It seemed like whenever she got a customer done, two more would appear at the end of the line.

A couple of hours later, the store closed and finally, *finally,* the line was gone. Relieved, I made my way over to help her gather up her purse and all the goodies—cakes, snippings of plants—that her readers had brought her. Her spirits were high and because I thought we were leaving, so were mine. That's when one of the store people wheeled out a dolly loaded with boxes of books for 'Tine to sign for later sale.

I was a little disappointed but when an author signs store stock they usually just sign a name, so I figured it would be a short delay at worst—until she started talking to her bookstore friends. In between every book, every *stock* book, she'd talk as if she were doing an individual autograph.

"You're *talking* more than you're *signing!*"—the ungrateful words slipped from my mouth.

I knew I had hurt her feelings and I felt bad about it; in fact, I still haven't gotten over it. If she'd been in a mood to bite, she might have told me to hush up and remind me just where her income came from—but what she did was worse. She got that tired, sad, dejected look which was harder on me to look at than being beaten with a stick.

❦ At the Southern Festival of the Book in Nashville one year, I got tired of everyone coming up to me interested in how I was 'Tine's granddaughter but not particularly interested in the fact that I had a book of my own. People just couldn't see past who I was biologically speaking.

"When I die," I told her sassily, "they're going to carve on my tombstone *Here lies Celestine Sibley's granddaughter.*" She loved that line. She loved it so much that that's how she began to introduce me over and over and over.

Throughout the years, I've had many people tell me how much they envy me, how easy my beginnings as a writer must have been because I'm my grandmother's granddaughter. And it would be honest to admit, though I'd rather not, that there were people who said there was some kind of competition going between me and my grandmother.

I remember the first signing for my debut book. I took my sons. We were standing outside the bookstore, my nervousness infecting the boys.

"What is it going to be like?" my oldest, nine-year-old Vincent, asked. "Like when 'Tine signs books?"

"You mean long lines and tons of people?" I asked, puffing on a cigarette.

"Yeah, like that," Vincent said completely confident that his mother would be lucky enough to be in such a situation.

"Nothing like 'Tine's signings," I said tensely. "I'll be lucky if anyone shows up. It'll probably just be me sitting at a table alone with my books."

Vincent thought a moment. "Don't compare yourself," he said matter-of-factly. "We'll just market and advertise."

✺ Somehow, even if you don't want to or mean to, it's hard to be in the same business as a successful family member and not compare yourself to that person. If I had been raised in a normal family in which no one was a writer, I think it would have been easier. When I was just starting out, not even my own mother took me seriously, let alone encouraged me. Even when I'd had three books with my name on them—by no means best-sellers—and was paying all of my considerable bills by freelancing, Mom offered that maybe I should go back to school until I figured out what I *really* wanted to do.

✺ Early on in my publishing career, there was a flurry of interest in "grandmother-granddaughter signings." I was easily taken in, only to show up and realize, it wasn't me they'd wanted at all—not even the two of us—just my grand-mother. At the last such dual signing, I went to the store to find the line in front of her side of the signing table leading out the door, a huge poster behind her chair, and posters with her likeness on them in the windows. At my side of the table there was a humiliating little stack of one of my chil-dren's books, a solitary chair, and not a single person waiting. I made a quick excuse about not feeling well. After that, when I got one of those sweet grandmother-granddaughter solici-tations, I gave them the number of 'Tine's office and, as politely as possible, said if they wanted her, to call her.

A handful of my grandmother's fans had heard 'Tine might be accompanying me to a signing for my children's book, *How to Rock Your Baby*, a book I'd worked really hard on. When we walked into the bookstore, they were waiting for her. Without a second thought, she sat down behind my signing table and began signing her own books.

I tried to run and hide in the car—cowardly, but there it is. When I got dragged back into the bookstore, I simply sat on the opposite side of the table and waited for someone to come up with my book. I felt like an impostor or an unwelcome guest. It's the kind of circumstance that rattles your confidence.

But I got through it and many other instances almost exactly the same. The moral for me was that she was who she was through no fault of my own and she was a damn good grandmother. And eventually, after a while, it got to the point where we were in cahoots. Me and 'Tine became comfortable going into a place together as a team.

✃ If you've ever been around books or authors, then you probably are aware that there's a great deal of competition and ego—and lots of testosterone—in the publishing world. When it comes down to it, I learned, it's far better to compare yourself to others, than it is with your own flesh and blood.

One season there was an Atlanta author who was as pleased as punch with himself. He showed up everywhere—on panels, at readings, at conventions, and holiday book sales.

I'd been at a couple of the same events as he but he never even spoke to me, in spite of the fact, I figured, he had to know who I was—the world just isn't that big. My grandmother had out-signed him in one town by maybe a hundred books. I was nervous about appearing at one particular event (I was the youngest and the only children's author invited) and there he was, blowing out hot air about how wonderful he was and how butter wouldn't melt in his mouth.

That's when I truly was benefitted by being my grandmother's granddaughter. The organizers of the event had the anthology of her work I'd edited, *The Celestine Sibley Sampler*, and her fans were afoot. I signed the sampler and I signed my own books. I wouldn't have cared if I was signing the Holy Bible. I signed until everyone else had gone to lunch. I signed with the single-mindedness of an animal in heat.

As soon as I could get to a phone, I called my grandmother. "I *out-signed* him!" I said gleefully, out of breath. "I had to sign your books—I was very nice to your customers—and I signed my books, but he was eating while I was still signing!"

"Good girl!" came the enthusiastic reply, and she meant it. Then she wanted to hear all the details. She had no patience for people who got pompous and self-important and she could listen to such small victories over the egotistical, petty though they were, with genuine interest.

I was blue before a signing at a book convention and 'Tine was worried that I wouldn't have enough spine. We were eating breakfast with Margaret Quinlin from Peachtree Publishers and 'Tine mulled me over with dissatisfaction. "I'm just worried that Sibley is the kind of author who would melt if she didn't have a line."

My head was down as I was signing at a low table later that day, so I couldn't see how long the line was. The books were giveaways but it was the longest line I ever had. Margaret walked by with 'Tine on the way to my grandmother's own signing and said, "I wish Sibley could see how many people there are—"

❧ I was asked to give a talk to a sort of golden age group at a church and I could just tell they weren't going to hear a word I had to say—they were wanting to fawn over my betters. I thought, I'll just nip that in the bud, I'll tell them a certain anecdote and that'll shut 'em up.

I related how once I was storytelling at an historic house when a woman came up to me and said, "Aren't you Sibley Fleming?"

"Why yes, I am," I'd said, straightening up my shoulders.

"I just love your grandmother," the woman had said.

Course as soon as I said *I just love your grandmother*, the old geezers took a breath in unison, as if they were a school of fish darting together in the same direction, and said, "*We do too!*"

❧ In 1995, on the way back from a book signing at Serendipity Book Store in McDonough, Georgia, 'Tine told me that she'd scheduled a doctor's appointment to have a lump in her breast examined. The lump turned out to be part of the cancer which later metastasized to different lymph nodes throughout her body. Her doctor, Martin York, saw her through the cancer and the grueling chemotherapy treatments.

The whole family was scared. My mother, who lived next door to my grandmother, shouldered the bulk of the burden of her care. I met 'Tine and Mom for doctors' appointments and chemotherapy sessions whenever I could. There were many nights during which I doubted my grandmother's ability to survive. I'm not sure how to express this, but as bad as it was and even at the times my grandmother hinted that she couldn't take another bout of chemo, I never believed that the cancer would get her.

After the cancer went into remission in 1996, 'Tine began the slow process of getting her strength back, a period of time through which she never let up on her book or work schedules.

✻ Books are like lovers but they will not keep you warm at night. Maybe it was having someone to share my life with, to love me whether my books were selling or not that wore me down as much as anything else about finally getting married, which I did in the summer that the Olympic Games were held in Atlanta, the summer of 1996.

Life in downtown Atlanta changed dramatically during the Olympics. You couldn't get in the *AJC* offices without a full body search. Cars were stopped at checkpoints and searched for potential bombs or terrorists. The city got a facelift. Hotels and restaurants were overflowing—business had never been so good.

For a couple months I'd been calling an old college friend who lived in Denver and Ron Letcher, who had also attended Centenary College with us, was his roommate. Ron and I ended up talking frequently by virtue of the fact that he often answered the phone.

In college, I'd had the worst crush on Ron—such a bad crush that whenever he entered a room, I nervously exited.

So our relationship evolved over the telephone for the first time fourteen years after I'd left college, and in June 1996, he came to Atlanta to see me. A little over two months later, we eloped. My grandmother was less than thrilled, in spite of the fact that Ron said dating me was as easy and comfortable as spending time with one of his cousins. Also, 'Tine had missed my first wedding and had wanted my second to be in her church, Roswell Presbyterian.

However, before long, my grandmother and the boys were as much in love with Ron as I. He found his way to our hearts through our stomachs by cooking hot nutritious meals, and by insisting that I cut my working hours to under fifty hours a week. He escorted the two of us to our signings, and patiently sat through countless industry dinners—many of which he catered.

Unfortunately, since there was no wedding ceremony, the first chance I had to meet Ron's family was at the wake for his sister's husband who had passed away unexpectedly. I was terrified. What could Ron's relations possibly think of me? I was a single mother with two children, divorced—I hadn't stopped for a formal ceremony or familial blessing. We had simply gone to the Atlanta probate court, he in shorts and me in a sundress, and asked the judge to tie the knot.

I told my grandmother I was worried. "I'll go along and back you up and make a good show," she said.

It was a relief. I figured it would look better to my new Alabama in-laws if I showed up with some family, someone to assure them I wasn't a brazen hussy come out of the blue. Ron and I picked up 'Tine and we all went to the funeral home for the wake.

There was little to fret about. All of the Letchers—even under the difficult circumstances—were kind and welcoming. Of course they were there to grieve, not to socialize. Everything was going fine until some of the mourners started going up quietly to my grandmother to shake her hand and tell her how much they enjoyed her writing. Then the quiet few creeping up to her became a line.

When the service was over, the widow, Ron's sister Cindy, said she didn't know how her poor dead husband would feel about being upstaged at his own wake.

When I told my grandmother, she was a little embarrassed at the idea of outshining a corpse. "That's silly," she scoffed.

So we didn't have a wedding or any parties, but when Ron came into our lives, I think it gave 'Tine some relief—the knowledge that I wouldn't be alone anymore.

✂ When my grandmother got sick for the last time, Ron told me not to worry about working—we'd nip and tuck our finances and I could do whatever she needed. He fixed faucets, patched roofs, painted walls in our house, and brought stability to my frantic existence. In the last month of her life, when she was in the hospital and wasn't communicating, Ron walked into her room and a big smile came over her face. I have never loved him more than I did in that moment—he treated her so kindly and with such respect. During that same hospitalization, he even did duty for me one night and she let him take care of her. Afterwards, she insisted Ron was one of her boys.

CHAPTER SEVEN

Gardeners, I am convinced, do not see the world in the same light as other folks. It was from earthful meanderings with my grandmother that I was steeped in the art of noticing. Through her eyes, all things came together in the garden—life, death, beauty, God, duty, patience, perseverance, awe, history, wealth, love, defeat— *everything*. For my grandmother, a garden was the place to build relationships with children because her own small children had shared her natural curiosity and wonder.

One of Bird's and my earliest projects with 'Tine was making terrariums. Terrariums can be likened to miniature worlds. If you were a ladybug, a terrarium would be a whole forest without much sky.

'Tine scouted around for containers first—under the cabinets in the kitchen, out under the eaves of the tool shed— and came up with a number of options to begin. There was a cute old blue bottle from her collection over the sink, mayonnaise and canning jars, and a giant pickle jar with a lid. The smaller the container, the less likely the project is to succeed—we found out by trial and error.

The bottom of your terrarium should be filled with moss, any color or kind. Between the seams of the pieces of moss, add seedling plants you find in the woods. There may be some kind of growth-stunting that goes on in the space of a terrarium—as with bonsai trees. Baby ferns tend to stay babies, as will heart-shaped ginger. If you poke a few holes in the top of your jar and water lightly, a terrarium will act as its own environment with the moisture evaporating, condensing on the sides of the container, and then raining back down onto the landscape. This can go on for months without your lifting a finger.

My grandmother behaved like a Tibetan monk when it came to saving plants. In her greenhouse, and outside its door, she ran a plant hospital for neglected greenery, tender babies bitten by frost or trampled by dogs. She'd water her patients, often re-pot them, talk to them, and nurture them until they "perked up a bit."

The irony is that after all the healing she'd performed, she'd inevitably have to go out of town for work and the person she designated to water—usually a child—would water lightly and only on the surface of the plants and all but the most hardy would shrivel up and die.

I do not know where she got the practice, but 'Tine was big on draping hanging baskets from trees—especially baskets of ferns. At a nearly hidden nursery across the river from her cabin she'd find huge, healthy ferns that looked like they came from a rain forest or the *Land of the Lost*. And, though she hated lending them, her conviction about hanging ferns improving the appearance of a porch in town made her go against her natural instincts.

Whenever I had a party or company coming, I could count on her showing up in the driveway, green tendrils lapping out of her trunk like spaghetti noodles dangling over the edge of a pot.

"Don't forget to water them," she'd shake her finger, "*every* day." She watered before she went to work, a hose in one hand and a cup of coffee in the other, using the time to inspect and note new growth, pull a weed, make mental notes of pests and strangling vines. Then when she got home from work, she'd slip out of her office clothes and into something loose, and she'd walk the yard over again with a beer.

There were times that I was bitter about those borrowed ferns, knowing that I was going to kill them out of neglect and that I'd never hear the end of it. Of course, that didn't stop her bringing them and, eventually, I did have enough time to get all of my watering done.

❦ It was in my late twenties that I discovered the value of planting native species—once you get them going, there's not a lot you can do to stop them. It was a tip I picked up the day The Garden Man, Lee May, showed up with 'Tine to consult over my yard like two surgeons discussing a patient. Lee could probably make a rock bloom—as my grandmother could have.

In my garden there was one troublesome flower bed set off by beautiful ancient cobblestones and a brick path, but also filled with an arrangement of bits of cement and dirt and the leaves of about ten shade trees.

"Hostas . . . native Georgia ferns . . . columbine . . . that's what you need there," Lee said. 'Tine nodded.

I'm sure they'll look great washing away with the first light rain, was all I could think. As if reading my mind, Lee, the guru, said, "Topsoil—plenty of topsoil."

The following Sunday morning when me and the boys arrived at Sweet Apple, my grandmother was still in church.

Not to let anything get in the way of my true mission—
COLLECTING FERNS—I put our Sunday dinner roast in
the oven and tidied up lest she feel compelled towards any
other task.

But there was no reason to worry. As soon as she got home,
she was out of her church clothes and into tennis shoes in no
time. To me, she looked sophisticated, nay, stunning with a
lovely old shovel in hand. We went into the woods that sloped
behind her cabin down to a little creek. On the way, we passed
the spot where she'd kept her honeybees and the remnants of
a clearing she and Jack had made once upon a time. There was
still a stump bench sitting solitary in the woods, slowly melt-
ing into the forest floor. Their idea had been to make a quiet
spot in which to sit and meditate in the mornings.

Too, by the creek where wild ferns grew, we saw the place
where Bird and I had attempted to dig a swimming hole only
to be thwarted by the fact that the particular creek which was
to feed it dries up with the first missed rainfall. Through
thickets of briars and poison ivy, 'Tine and I looted and pil-
laged the fertile banks, emerging with two garbage bags full
of fronds—both the regular variety of Georgia fern and the
Christmas tree kind.

Sensing my lust for native plants (and perhaps wanting to
encourage it), my grandmother advocated a trip to Holly
Creek in the mountains for more of the same. There she
commented, as I happily dug and separated the roots of ferns
from their native dirt, that she'd never seen so many ferns
displaced at one time.

But by then, I was already planning another flower bed on
the other side of the house.

Transplanting in and of itself is a whole other issue. I had
luck once getting some wild Dorothy Perkins roses out of the

bank across the road from Sweet Apple and into the yard of a lady of the same maiden name, but that was pure luck.

'Tine loved attempting transplanting and wished that the Queen Anne's Lace in her country neighborhood would be happy holding court in her front yard, specifically in the flower beds she dug up by her front steps and partitioned off with a low grey picket fence in the English style.

Lyniece Talmadge, a good friend of mine, called one day to tell me she was dividing her garden. There were old-fashioned daylilies that bloom bright yellow, clumps of red hot pokers, gladiola, and vinca minor, all of which needed a new home. I could have all the plants I could carry, she said, if I would just come and pick them up.

"Free plants!" my grandmother exclaimed. "Take off work and go get them." She then added a couple of lines about watering the holes before I planted, planting in the cool of the day, and not leaving the hand-me-downs out of the ground and forgetting about them until it was too late.

I didn't have a lot of faith in my ability to successfully transplant so much flora but it wasn't an opportunity I was going to pass up on at least trying.

The surgery was completed a day later and the patients, sad and droopy, recovered in intensive care. There were so many of them, however, I realized greedily, that if even half lived, I had just filled two huge flower beds with annuals that I could never afford. It was possible I could forget the word *perennial* that season.

After ferns, my next want was a blue rose bush. Me and 'Tine were at a Woolworth's where there were little cylindrical packages of roses on sale for about two dollars a piece. She was inspecting yellow Peace roses the color of cream, deep red roses, and ladified miniature sweetheart pinks. I had a blue rose bush package with the canes sticking out of the top. The picture of the bush in bloom was thrilling. A blue rose—why, it must be good luck, I thought.

"Put that down," my grandmother told me. "You don't want that."

"But it's *blue*—" I said.

"Unnatural and tacky," she sniffed. "We thought Muv would die if she didn't get one when they first came out."

"Did she get her blue rose bush?"

"Finally—but I think it died."

'Tine was against that blue rose bush as much as she was against the color purple in gardens. Her rule that anything that blooms is beautiful just didn't apply there. And I relate this story not to compare my taste with 'Tine's because my grandmother's taste was irreproachable on most subjects. I tell this story to make a point: gardening is as personal a thing as choosing a hairstyle or the clothes on your back.

Shopping with my grandmother often entailed finding out what I liked by virtue of learning what *she* liked. In her book, daylilies were a scam. They took up a lot of space and only bloomed once a year. St. John's Wort was a weed that multiplied so prolifically in the wild (and in her yard), that only the most foolhardy gardener would pay for the privilege of having it. I paid.

In addition to wildflowers, my grandmother believed in Confederate jasmine and Lady Bankshire roses. She didn't warm up to roses until late in life, thinking that they needed lots of care and expensive pesticides. By the time she did, she already had so many natural pesticides in her garden—mint, rosemary, and other herbs—that her roses actually did quite well.

Anyway, when shopping with 'Tine, when you finally found something that *she* approved of, the rule was to get *three*—that was the magic number. The reasoning is that if one doesn't make it, then there are two others to step into the front line. Three will also make a show of color whereas one is easily obscured.

Every time I shopped without her, on my own, she took it as an affront if—because I could often barely afford *one*—I didn't always get *three*. Too, I was no doubt making frivolous decisions without the counsel of my betters.

When I first began gardening as an adult, I could almost never afford to buy anything. After my marriage, things got easier and I could make cautious trips to a hardware store or nursery without breaking the bank.

I would have done better to listen to my betters and have, as in other areas of life, made many mistakes by not accepting existing wisdom. I did, however, want moon flowers like 'Tine's which opened like large white disks in the evening at her house, her wildlife theater. Where I made my mistake was in thinking that if I planted numerous seed packets of morning glories (a colorful kudzu substitute), I would not only have an evening show but one in the morning as well. My grandmother let me go forward with this idea, probably gazing out the window at the raisin vine which in her youth she had purposely planted, but which by then covered the well house, the rhododendrons that Jack got her, and the boxwood, before it strung its way up to the top of the pines. But she didn't give me a raisin vine-type hint. She didn't stop me. She just nodded as if I'd come up with an original, interesting scheme.

Then the morning glories began roaming over my new picket fence, over the roses and over the arbor that Vincent built for me. They spread out—all over the place like a giant Chia Pet. It was hard to get through the front gate without being mulled over by the morning glories. And the moon flowers? We enjoyed all two of them immensely. Growing morning glories with moonflowers to have blooms both morning and evening wasn't a plan I was going to repeat. I told 'Tine this and she said wryly, "You don't have to—they reseed themselves."

It didn't matter though, not really. 'Tine was pleased because gardening had become an addiction with me. Gardening addiction is when your hands get all sweaty and no matter what is going on, you're always on the road to a nursery plotting how to get free yellow flagstone out of Alabama road cuts and lusting after birdbaths, windmills, and other gardening accouterments. It's when your favorite magazine (at least for Southerners) becomes *Southern Living* and you don't care who knows it.

You know you are a gardening addict when you find you do not need groceries, new shoes, or gas in the car—the most pressing necessity becomes an oak-leaf hydrangea or some of that blue plumbago that has just arrived at the local nursery.

A gardening addict has grand and lofty thoughts. My grandmother once wanted an all-white garden out on her patio and slowly she began hacking away at this dream, pulling together different shapes and smells and blossoms as if all white flowers flocked together like clouds.

She often got tickets to the annual Atlanta Flower Show which, while enlightening, is also a humbling jaunt—the place where you discover how much there is you don't know, how much there is you haven't done, and how much there is you could do if you were a millionaire. At least that's how I always came away from it. My grandmother, on the other hand, saw what ideas she'd had on her own, what she'd done better, and, as if stealing national secrets, she came away with inspiration even if she didn't drop a penny buying from the exhibits.

Still, flower shows anywhere serve as markers of the approach of spring and are like a Grand Opening in a gardener's life, the World Series of the green thumbs, the Super Bowl of blossoms.

As spring approaches, the sun seems to take its time as it drops toward the horizon. It takes its time sloping to the city skyline, takes its time to touch the rolling bright green grass. The color of the sunset is not the dull winter hue but more of a rich butter yellow that blends with the blue clouds like a layered dessert. The curtains of light drop on the sky and the street lamps become the dominant feature. People are rushing in their cars, piling up behind red lights as if driving is only made possible by rain.

You begin to notice things. Though the oak trees are still bare, a Japanese magnolia has had the impertinence to flounce its pink pompoms way too soon. It is too beautiful to lay blame upon.

Daffodils, the dumbest plants I've ever come across, poke up through the dirt, their long green arms fragile cradles of bloom. And you think their babies will freeze.

A true gardener will worry over daffodils and their irresponsible nature, wonder how many azaleas will return, try to imagine that the dogwoods are casting petals of snow over the brown earth, and that the sun—*finally*—is actually hot enough to burn her nose.

Driving away from the flower show, 'Tine would sing joyfully a poem to her own music:

If you have but two pence
Buy a loaf of bread and a hyacinth!

As my husband Ron and I were moving into our new house in in East Point, a suburb south of Atlanta, in 1998, we arrived home late one afternoon to find on the porch a green vase full of cut old-fashioned pink roses, a box of impatiens, little plastic pots of nicotiana and lemon mint, a fledgling vine that makes purple pea pods, and a cardboard box lid loaded with strawberry plants. 'Tine left nothing so mundane as a hot meal, sheets for the windows, or dishwashing liquid.

Ron was not amused. He comes from a practical background. Having grown up in the country in Alabama, his family ate out of vegetable gardens, drank milk from an aunt's cow, and in general managed the land skillfully. His grandfather had owned most of Blount County, Alabama, and left the majority of his land to the sharecroppers who'd worked the soil, a complete understanding of the honest ways of ownership.

Here now, 'Tine and me and an example of our upside-down logic. Ron's and my "new" house, built in 1903, had a leaky roof and faulty wiring. My grandmother dropped by on our move-in day to do a little renovation—*her way.* Put flowers out and paint the dirt around the front door—that's how you fix a place up. So as Ron was carrying beds and boxes into the house on his back, he was stumbling over her extended legs as she sat on the porch directing me. It was important that I know what to put in the ground, what to put in a pot and where to put it.

🦋 Mother's Day 1999, came and Vincent built me a potting table. I am very lucky in that my oldest child is skillful with tools and is not afraid to tackle a project scrawled in the air by his mother. My children know that my favorite presents from them are the thoughtful homemade type, even though

Vincent pointed out that the material and paint would be far more expensive, more than a bottle of lotion from the drugstore. Like I cared.

My grandmother, she was the same. When she looked at the new potting table that Vincent had built me, she saw in her mind an empty space in her greenhouse where a potting table wasn't.

"When you gonna come out and work for me?" she asked her eldest great-grandson.

Turning to me, she said, "You're not going to leave that on your front porch, are you?"

"Why wouldn't I? I'm proud of it and I do most of my repotting and seed-starting on the porch anyway."

"Because it doesn't go there. You want people to see all your junk—your gloves and plant food and seed packets?"

"I don't care if they do. Maybe I could sell them one of Vincent's potting tables—they could see how handy they are."

"Do you not have a place to put it?"

"Yeah, on the front porch."

"I mean a place to hide it—it's for working, not for showing off."

"I'm happy to show it off," I said finally. "I'm not moving it."

My grandmother was, as usual, on her way to work. She craned her head scanning the distance, one foot in the car, and said, "What about back behind the house? There must be a place there."

But I never moved it. It doesn't sound big on the surface but let me tell you, it is a damned recognizable rite of passage when you don't move your potting table just because your grandmother told you to.

I've no doubt that her penchant for English murder mysteries and English gardens was passed on to me like a birthmark. After the potting table episode and a new picket fence (my grandmother liked the old metal one and all the vines that came with it), I decided I wanted a Prince Charles garden. With English lavender all along the front walk on either side, thick and purple and fragrant.

'Tine lauded my enthusiasm, noting at the same time with sinister glee, "I've never had much luck with lavender."

I wanted lavender but instead she dropped off an old chipped white enamel bucket full of leggy zinnias wrapped in damp newspaper. They were a gift from a neighbor and 'Tine had planted all she cared to revive. The stalks were thick and dry and the weight from the top to the roots was so heavy, I couldn't see exactly what they were going to do in my burgeoning English garden.

"Clip them down," she said, shaking her head. "Mine don't look very good either but maybe they'll come back and bloom again."

I am not so prideful that I would let misshapen Quasimodo-type zinnias die just because they are not show quality. I resented having them take up newly turned earth and all that fertilizer, oh my good manure.

But here's what happened. The English lavender, which I found myself at nurseries all over town, got some disease, turned brown and scraggly, and died. The offending zinnias shortly thereafter bloomed in pink, red, and orange. The next bed over, I planted two rows of giant yellow sunflowers. 'Tine nodded her head in agreement, *genuine* agreement. The way the colors offset each other and blended, and the flowers' heights, textures, and enthusiasm toward life, almost made my modest patch look like the beginnings of an English garden.

CHAPTER EIGHT

My children will tell you gladly that their mother is no cook. My brother Bird, who is an excellent chef, says it's not that I *can't* cook, it's that I *won't* cook, but oddly enough, the result is the same.

Once, I was expanding upon my repertoire of scorched meals, burnt breads, and two ingredient recipes. I doubled the yeast in a bread recipe and the bread machine exploded—the adage "if once is good, twice is nice" doesn't actually apply to cooking.

"Don't brag about what you can't do," my grandmother once scolded me.

"But I'm a terrible cook," I said as someone else might say they have small feet.

"No, you're not. You just don't get any practice," 'Tine said, getting that annoyed, dismissive look. If she had been a hand-slapper, mine would have been slapped.

"Okay. I don't get any practice because I'd rather be digging ditches than standing in a kitchen. It's the most boring thing in the world I can think to do. You stand over the stove and stare at something until you can't stare anymore. The minute you go out of the room, it burns and then no one eats it anyway," I came back.

"That may be, Miss Priss, but *Muv* always said you shouldn't take pride in your shortcomings."

✄ Part of the reason my grandmother was considered such a good cook was simply that she *was*. The other part had to do with the pleasure and attention she brought to even the most insignificant meal. She nurtured her collection of napkins, plates, and silverware and she didn't wait for spring or a florist delivery to get fresh flowers for the centerpiece. She'd pull dried flowers and berries together if necessary.

'Tine had an almost religious reverence for food and for mealtime. Eating in front of the television simply never happened at her house unless it was late-night ice cream. Even eating on the porch didn't mean eating from your lap. Meals in the living room and on the porch were punctuated with candlelight. On the porch, she had old wooden spools of different heights that doubled as candleholders, and over the formal table hung an iron chandelier with either white or red candles, depending on the season. Though nearly all of her decorations came from junk stores and the occasional yard sale, she had such a unique sense of style and eye for arranging that her tables put even Martha Stewart to shame.

There may have been a time—now clean from my memory—but I don't recall ever sitting down without asking the blessing. Usually, when children were present, she'd designate the most willing to say "God is great, God is good, let us thank him for our food. By his hands we are fed, he gives to us our daily bread. *Amen.*"

If there was company, she would ask one of the guests to say a blessing. One favorite I heard was from Reverend

Patricia Templeton, a dear friend and associate past
Timothy's Episcopal Church on Signal Mountain, Te
(In 1997, Patricia had led the prayer at the cere
which my grandmother accepted the Shining Light Award
given by the Atlanta Gas Light Company, a gas lamp that
burns eternally in front of the offices of the *Atlanta Journal-Constitution*.) She and her husband, Joe Monti, had come for
lunch at Sweet Apple in early December of 1998. It was just
the four of us.

Patricia bowed her head, saying, "Thank you for food that
feeds our bodies and friends who feed our hearts."

As we raised our heads and began passing dishes around
the table, 'Tine ventured, "I know you're good at prayers,
Patricia, but how are you at funerals?"

"Why are we talking about this?" Patricia asked quietly.

"I want to commission you to do mine."

It was unsettling conversation. For once in my life, I
remained silent, fiddling with my silverware, self-consciously
slathering butter on my bread. I did not know at that point
how sick 'Tine was.

❦ Patricia Templeton had been my grandmother's "young
friend" for a quarter of a century. 'Tine was fiercely proud of
Patricia and did not skimp on her loyalty to her. They had
been friends since Patricia was eighteen years old and she'd
boldly requested an interview with my grandmother for a
high school paper she was writing.

"For twenty-five years we were friends; she was like a
touchstone for me. If I needed to talk, I could always call her
and talk things over. I didn't feel like there was anything I
could do in return. I remember calling her when I was thinking about going into the Peace Corps, wondering how it
would affect my career," Patricia said.

No doubt deeming the Peace Corps an institution in which heroes are made, 'Tine's solid advice was, "You've *got* to do it."

But before the Peace Corps; before working as an editor at the *Nashville Banner* covering politics and general assignments; before she'd put herself through divinity school at the University of the South in Sewanee, Tennessee; as an undergraduate Patricia had been a reporter for the *Red and Black*, the student newspaper of the University of Georgia in Athens.

"When Carter was elected president in 1976," Patricia recalled, "'Tine had been to the convention and covered some of the campaign in Plains and I was there for the *Red and Black* from UGA. She took me around with her to interview Billy Carter, Miss Lillian—everyone. She'd say, 'This is my friend Patricia, she's a reporter for the *Red and Black*'— like that was something. Carter was supposed to be coming into Plains the next morning but the *Red and Black* photographer had to be back for class—and he was taking the truck. She told me, of course, that I was going to miss class and she was going to drive me back to Athens."

When Patricia was ordained in 1994, 'Tine flew up to Nashville for the celebration and talked the maid at the Hermitage Hotel into letting her into Patricia's room.

"She took me out to lunch that day before the ordination," Patricia recalled. "She wanted to have a last meal with me before I got holy."

The next day in Atlanta, 'Tine fell to and wrote a column. It turned out that officials of the Sewanee school of theology decided at Patricia's graduation—ironically the first class that was fifty percent women—to give an honorary doctorate to a bishop who would not ordain women. Reverend Templeton countered by boycotting commencement. "'Tine loved that," Patricia told me. "She wrote about how proud she was."

❦ I'd like to share a few favorite recipes and craft projec
that we grandchildren enjoyed making with 'Tine. As muc
as the physical project, whether it was making cookies o
paper chains for the Christmas tree, it was the warmth and
magic she brought to the table that made every tidbit edible
and every simple craft grand.

❦ COMPANY BEEF STEW

*This stew is so good you can serve it to your minister or
your newspaper publisher. If you have leftovers, keep in
mind that 'Tine was strongly against animals eating
out of plates and pots and pans, so if any of your children share with your pets, give away the offending dish
to a relative who doesn't keep good house.*

*'Tine had a pewter pot that she'd heat by rinsing it
with boiling water before adding the stew to bring to
the table. (Remember that some people believe that
ingesting the lead from pewter pots, flatware, plates,
and such can cause derangement if used on a daily
basis.) Company beef stew is best served over rice with
crusty French bread and butter. A light salad is nice as
a first course.*

Package of beef stew pieces or better, get a nice, well-
    marbled roast (with enough fat to add
    to the broth)
2 large onions or a sack of pearl onions
Olive oil
Salt and pepper
Small bag of carrots or a one-pound bag of
    pre-peeled baby carrots, thickly sliced

2 whole garlic cloves (take out before you serve)
2-pound bag of potatoes, quartered
Big package of mushrooms, sliced
Bottle of red cooking sherry, red wine, or whatever is
   in your cabinet

Brown the meat and onions in a little bit of olive oil in an iron skillet. Add salt and pepper to taste. Dump browned beef and onions into a big stew pot and don't forget the drippings. Add water to cover, then add carrots, garlic, and potatoes. Simmer until you can easily get a fork into the hard vegetables, but not until they are too soft.

When you come to this point, you're ready to put in the mushrooms. My grandmother used a brush to brush the dirt off mushrooms as opposed to washing them. It's supposed to be better—worth a try. Last of all, flavor with red wine of your choice.

❧ All of my brothers are expert crabbers as are my sons. They're happy to bait a crab trap but the real excitement comes from stalking their prey in the late evening. The crabs at Dog Island (I'm sure like crabs everywhere) hide around old stumps, sunken boats, and seaweed. If you're out catching them on your own, or if your children are out with nets scooping them up out of the bay, here are a few tips. Firstly, it's good to remember that she-crabs cannot be taken when they are with eggs. That is the orange mass you see on their bellies when you flip them over. It is legal, however, if you have the stomach to do it, to take one claw and throw the expectant mother back into the water. Secondly, when crabbing you don't have to be quite as quiet as you would be if you were fishing, but still, creep up on them and *scoop!* When crabs are scarce, it can take a whole day to get enough for a meal for six—about twenty. Lastly, keep them in a cooler out of the sun and replenish their water with fresh sea water so they can breath. If you don't live near the sea, you can get crabs live and fresh at a farmer's market. I've looked it up lots of places and I doubt it would kill you to boil a newly deceased crustacean, but to be on the safe side, commit yourself to cooking only live ones.

❧ ISLAND BLUE CRAB BOIL

Small bag of new potatoes
6 ears of corn, cut in halves
1 package of crab boil
1 pound of salted butter
20 live blue crabs
4 fresh lemons
2 loaves crusty French bread

Boil your potatoes and corn with a sack of crab boil until done. Remove corn and potatoes to another pot. Cover the table in newspaper. Melt the butter slowly so that it doesn't burn. I don't like drawn butter, prepared by skimming all the solids off the top of melted butter, because it has all the salt taken out. Drop crabs into boiling water and boil for a few minutes until pink or red, depending on the crab. The sort of grayish orange stuff is fat and you can eat it. Cajuns consider it a delicacy.

Now, your guests will fall under one of two categories: those who know how to pick crabs and those who just don't feel all the effort is worth it. Give everyone a serrated steak knife and do a quick demonstration. First, you pull off the bottom plate starting with your thumb under the head, then remove the claws and legs. Wash your crab, taking off all the insides and fat and return to the table. Now you can break the body in half once more and you'll notice there are "knuckles" where each leg was. Cut between the knuckles with the serrated knife and expose the lump crab meat. Smashing the claws requires a hammer. Serve with lemon and French bread.

✂ My grandmother taught me to make her cornbread when I was living in a tiny apartment on Juniper Street in midtown Atlanta with baby Vincent. There is a noticeable proportion to the ingredients in the following recipe so you can make more or less, depending on the size of your skillet.

✂ 'TINE'S GOOD CORNBREAD

This particular cornbread ain't sweet—it's just right. Once I was making it to go with fresh vegetable soup and I'd invited Lee May, the garden and food writer and columnist for the AJC, *and my grandmother over to eat it. I've never seen two qualified chefs more interested in a batch of cornbread. As I dealt with each ingredient, they hovered over my bowl and conferred as if they were directing the dismantling of a bomb. The cornbread came out good—it always does if you follow the recipe. We ate it, slathered with butter, with soup in front of the fireplace.*

2 tablespoons bacon grease, Crisco, or lard
2 cups self-rising cornmeal
1 cup buttermilk
1 egg

Preheat the oven to 350°F. Put grease in an iron skillet and stick it in the oven to heat. Meanwhile, in a large mixing bowl gently turn cornmeal, buttermilk, and egg together using a wooden spoon. (If you don't have an egg, you don't need it. What the egg does is take away some of the dryness, makes the meal no-fool rise and adds some texture. If you're the type of cook who doesn't need a little extra guarantee, don't worry with the egg.) Do not overmix.

Test your skillet to see if the grease is hot enough. You can drop a dab of spit or a little water or batter and see if it sizzles. When the grease starts to hiss— don't burn yourself, get a big thick potholder—quickly pour the grease into your batter and mix rapidly. Immediately pour the batter into the skillet and place it in the oven until brown. If you have a strange oven, you can also let your cornbread cook until done, then brown the top under the broiler. Be careful though, it only takes a minute, so don't go read a book.

The following old family recipe was most likely from my grandfather Jim Little who died before I was born. 'Tine made it for us when we were small and so did my mother. It's a sort of Thursday-night dish, something to make out of what's left in the cupboard before you get your paycheck. It's cheap, hot, and good. You can substitute real corned beef for canned and doctor it up to suit your tastes, but it's really very nourishing just as is.

✄ DAGGERINI

1 can corned beef
1 large can whole tomatoes
1 onion, sliced
3 garlic cloves
Olive oil
Salt and pepper to taste
1 package pasta (shells, flat noodles, any kind works)

Put a large pot of water on to boil for the pasta. Open
the cans of corned beef and tomatoes and chop up the
onion and garlic. In a saucepan, lightly sauté the
corned beef, tomatoes, onion, and garlic in olive oil.
Salt and pepper to taste. Don't forget to put the pasta
in the water. When the pasta is done, mix it all
together, set the table, and feed your hungry babies.

✄ One of 'Tine's favorite stories was the one about stone soup
and I think the soup in the fable was the basis for the following
recipe. It'd sure be good if maybe you added an onion, even
better with a couple of potatoes. Stone soup is excellent with a
beef bone. Some carrots and tomatoes give it a little extra zip.

✄ TWO-DAY VEGETABLE BEEF SOUP

1 package soup bones
Okra
2 large cans whole tomatoes
1 can corn
5 large carrots, peeled and sliced
4 large potatoes

Handful dried pasta of choice
2 large onions, sliced

My grandmother always started her soup in a big pot
with a package of soup bones. Boiling the bones to make
the broth takes hours. She might also have purchased a
package of soup meat, depending on her mood and,
likely, her pocketbook. At night, when it's done, set the
soup out on the porch (covered so the animals don't get
it) to cool.

The next morning, skim off the fat and return the
pot of soup to the stove. Of course, the hope and prob-
ability is that the next morning happens to be Saturday
or Sunday so you can tinker with your soup all day
when you come in from the garden or the greenhouse.

✂ To be honest, one of the few things 'Tine didn't make well
was biscuits. When we were growing up, she kept canned biscuits in her refrigerator door but switched to the bagged,
Pillsbury kind later in life. For this reason, I am sharing my own
biscuit recipe below. It's one of the great ironies that while I am
not a natural cook, I can make really good biscuits. Having said
that, the key to cat head biscuits is to have the ingredients room
temperature, the kitchen warm, and use a light hand.

✂ CAT HEAD BISCUITS

4 tablespoons grease or butter
2 cups self-rising flour
1 cup buttermilk or whole milk
9 x 9-inch glass or metal pan

Preheat the oven to 350°F. As with cornbread, the idea is to melt the butter or bacon grease in the oven but you don't want to get it so hot that it passes the sizzle test. Melt your butter without boiling it and put the pan on the top of the stove to sit while you mix the rest. In a large bowl, add the flour (sifted is best but I never do that) and then the buttermilk.

You have to get a feel for how to mix the dough—probably the batter is better off gooey and full of air-holes than it is when it gets tight. Heavily flour your chopping block or table or whatever you cut out your biscuits on and carefully dump the batter into the center of the flour. Sprinkle the flour evenly around your batter and knead it carefully with the palm of your hand but not until it's elastic. Roll it out to about three-quarters of an inch thick and cut the biscuits with a wide-mouth cup or glass.

Handle each biscuit as you would a delicate newborn as you dip the top in the butter and then gently flip it over in the baking pan. The biscuits should be so close together that they are touching. Depending on where the rest of your breakfast is, you can either bake the biscuits immediately or cover them with a cotton cloth to rise. Baking time is about 20 minutes or until brown.

✄ With all due respect, my grandmother had nearly the same reverence for ambrosia as a priest does for communion bread. It was about as much a part of her idea of Christmas as having an angel on top of the tree. So have reverence when you make this.

✂ CHRISTMAS AMBROSIA

1/2 cup grapefruit sections
4 cups navel orange sections (about 1 dozen oranges)
1 cup pineapple
1/2 cup coconut shavings
1/2 cup chopped pecans

Making ambrosia requires perseverance. Basically, you peel and section the citrus fruits. You cut up the pineapple into chunks and then mix all the ingredients together. It's a good weekend project. Put it on the sideboard to show it off a few days ahead of your main meal if you have a cold house like a log cabin, if not, refrigerate it. That gives the ambrosia a chance to steep in its own juices.

Serve it from a cut crystal bowl that reflects the lights in the dining room. Don't use the bowl for anything else but this one dish once a year. On a realistic note, if you don't have crystal, cut glass can work—it's the thought that counts.

✂ My grandmother didn't like eggs. She'd had the misfortune as a child to sniff a rotten egg and while she'd cook them, she wouldn't eat eggs unless they were mixed into something else like a cake or a casserole. In spite of her distaste for eggs, she was careful to hide this fact from all children until they were grown and could make up their own minds. All of the other ingredients in the meal described below were her favorites.

✀ PICNIC BASKET
FOR JOHNSON'S ROCK

Bread
Butter
Honey
Tuna fish
Mayonnaise (Duke's)
Purple onion
Peanut butter
Very ripe bananas (just before rot sets in)
Apples
Thermos of coffee
Crackers and sardines
Boiled eggs

Pack some pretty cloth napkins in your picnic basket. Hike through the woods until you are starving. By this point, you have passed old dumps and toadstools, your pockets are bulging with mica rocks, and your hair is full of briars and thistles. Don't fall over the edge of Johnson's Rock. Watch the small children. Don't assume they heard you the first time. Lay out what's in your basket and you'll be surprised how good the sardines sit in your stomach.

✀ For the following recipe, you will need a ring mold (i.e., a round mold with a hole in the middle). If you have a garden, you're ahead of the game. If not, don't worry—all the ingredients are available at a decent grocery store or from your neighbor's garden. 'Tine primarily made the herb ice ring for parties, most notably, children's organized birthday parties.

And, really, "organized" in our family meant sending out invitations and cleaning up the house. There was never a strategy for what guests should or shouldn't do, no planned entertainment other than maybe a guitar player who knew three chords and some train songs. Anyhow, the ice ring adds a festive air to any bowl of punch.

✂ ICE RING MOLD

Good bunch of mint sprigs (any kind will do but
   lemon mint is nice if you can get it)
Small bunch of rosemary sprigs
1 lemon, sliced
1 orange, sliced
Jar of syrupy red cherries for color
Carton of lemonade

I think the way to put all of this together is fairly obvious. Pour the lemonade in the ring mold and then arrange your other items with artistic aplomb. Key is this, you don't have to use lemonade, although it adds flavor to the punch. You can make a heavier punch and use water for the ice ring and the ring will dilute the punch as it melts.

'Tine made this ice ring for Wolfie's fifth birthday. All of his preschool classmates had had wildly organized, high-profile children's parties with clowns and other such entertainment. There were designated drop-off and pick-up times.

So when it came to be Wolfie's turn to be honored with a party, me and 'Tine made an effort. We sent out invitations and strung up balloons and streamers across the front porch.

We made the ice ring, punch, and cake for the children, and coffee and muffins for the grownups, and waited for the guests to arrive. If the siblings of the invitees showed up, we told 'em to come on and stay. Then the parents stayed and drank coffee with us while the children played randomly in the yard, treehouse, and street. There was nothing planned, with the exception of the opening of the gifts which were many and grand. We were so pleased with our success as gracious hostesses—well, until Wolfie opened his last gift and turned to us, indicating the crowd.

"When are they going home?" he asked with a yawn.

✄ Forget all your troubles. Only the biggest fool can ruin the rice using the following recipe. It comes out so good that nobody believes how easy it is. That bit about putting rice in a pan then adding enough water to reach above your thumb knuckle is a crock (I've never done that when it didn't burn), so take heed and do what I say here.

✄ 'TINE'S PERFECT STEAMED RICE

You need a big pot, the kind that you could fit a whole bag of potatoes into or say, a full-size strainer. This recipe doesn't deal with measurements, thank God, as I don't own any measuring cups. I think the measure of a cook is not his cooking implements but his ability to feel his way around the kitchen. Anyway, you can make too much if you forget that, when cooked, rice swells up several times its size when dry. So, keep that in mind. Or plan on rice pudding or chicken bog for the next several days.

Using a discerning eye, pour an amount of rice into your big pot and cover as high as you can with water— you don't want to put so much water in there that it might boil over. Key being, you want enough water to insure that your rice can't burn. What you're going to do is turn the burner on high—gas is best—and boil the rice until it's just beginning to get cooked, but is not cooked through.

Then, take your strainer and pour the rice into it in the sink. Run cold water over the rice to rinse it. You can use a paper towel or you can use a cotton cloth but either way, it goes over the rice.

Fill your big pot with water about halfway. Put the strainer with the rice in it on top of the pot. Bring the water to boil and steam the rice to completion. This is really good rice—the best.

❧ In my grandmother's opinion, there was nothing worse than overly sweet, gooey cake products. (She was also disdainful of "wet" sandwiches that had too much "goop.") As a result, there weren't many over-the-counter muffins that she could be plied with, and certainly not any banana breads. A goodie was something that should be only slightly moist because it went with coffee and the two complimented each other.

One of treats she really loved was Ellen Howle's banana bread, precisely because it is not at all gooey. No matter how annoyed she might be with "us girls" or how skeptical she was about our current plot to take over the world, seeing us standing at her back door she'd catch Ellen's eye, peering suspiciously under her visitor's arm and ask, "What'd you bring me?" She'd welcome that covered loaf of banana bread in one smooth motion—from Ellen to the chopping block, unwrap the tin foil, and then slice it thickly and offer it around before we had our coats off.

What I'd do was, on my cleaning day which was once a week, I'd take Ellen and one of her banana breads with me to Sweet Apple. My grandmother and Ellen would sit on the front porch entertaining each other while I slaved away with Endust and mops and vacuums. This was good in a way because I could clean without hindrance and, if there was any notion of a trip to the grocery store, the nursery, or the Goodwill, they could go it alone without me. See, when you're cleaning for a person who's home, they have a tendency to follow you around, pointing out dirt and lifting up items to be dusted under. They want to know what you scrubbed and how long a break you're taking. They want to talk to you but then they want to blame you for slothfulness when you stop to talk to them. Just don't do it.

I do not know if a recipe is an appropriate forum to discuss occupation but, for the record, I must mention that I really was not a qualified housekeeper and furthermore, I tried to quit but numerous times. When I told my grandmother I was throwing in the towel, she'd tell me she didn't want anyone else, she'd just do it herself. So, I pretty much kept the job until she died. I was a freelance cleaning lady with one customer.

❧ CLEANING-DAY BANANA BREAD

1 cup sugar
1/2 cup butter
3 very ripe bananas

2 eggs
2 cups sifted flour
1 teaspoon salt
3/4 cup walnuts, chopped
1 teaspoon vanilla

Preheat oven to 350°F. Cream sugar and butter together.
Add mashed bananas and eggs. Sift dry ingredients
together and add to the creamed mixture. Add walnuts.
Add vanilla. Bake in a greased loaf pan for one hour.
Ellen says if the oven's not preheated, the bread will rise
flat. If you don't add the nuts, it'll come out mushy.
Don't skimp on the bananas, hell, add more. And finally,
Ellen's banana bread is excellent frozen, then thawed,
reheated, and served with a dollop of butter or cream
cheese.

🐾 Now, I know that my grandmother learned to eat the particular navy bean soup in the recipe following while covering
stories in Washington, D.C., for the *AJC*. It may or may not be
the way they make it in the senate commissary and it may or
may not be what they serve to the senators. Either way, it's good
on a cold day served with cornbread. You can put all of the
ingredients together in a Crock-Pot or slow cooker before you
go to work and simmer the mixture on low for the rest of the
day so you have a soothing, hot meal when you get home. Or
you can make it on the weekend and feed whoever is doing yard
work or working on a big project for you as they get hungry.

✄ 'TINE'S SENATORS' NAVY BEAN SOUP

1 package white navy beans
2 thick slices of ham with fat, chopped
2 tablespoons vegetable oil
3 or 4 large carrots, peeled and chopped
2 large potatoes, skinned and chopped
1 chicken bullion cube
2 medium onions, chopped
Salt and pepper

Soak the beans overnight for the best results. There are "quick cook" soaking methods but they are not nearly as reliable. Often the beans come out crunchy or they get to that twilight zone where they will never get done no matter how much heat or fat you apply to them. First, cook your beans with the ham and vegetable oil until they are tender. Then, add carrots, potatoes, bullion cube, and onions and cook until the potatoes have dissolved and made a sort of thick broth. Salt and pepper to taste.

✄ Nutmeg is the key ingredient in the following recipe for fruit tarts. See, once upon a time (i.e., in my grandmother's childhood), nutmeg was about as common a spice for fruit as cinnamon is today. It's an acquired taste if you didn't get it early on, but one worth grabbing hold of. Tart fruit is best for cooking because it can be sweetened with sugar and it tends to have a denser texture than sweet fruit. 'Tine made these tarts with sour green apples, as I recall, but you could use nearly any kind of fruit.

Now, the truth is, if you're not into flouring up your kitchen, you can buy pre-made pastry dough and it'll probably taste as good (or better) than anything you could make. My grandmother, however, enjoyed the process and most of the time, she really did attempt her own pastry dough. She kept a pastry cloth that always had flour on it and she'd roll up her rolling pin inside it before she tucked it away in a drawer.

❦ FRUIT TARTS WITH NUTMEG

4 tart apples, peeled and sliced
Juice of 1 fresh lemon
1/2 teaspoon salt
1-1/4 cups sifted self-rising flour
2 sticks unsalted butter, chilled
1 tablespoon hot water
1 cup sugar
Whole fresh nutmeg, grated

Preheat oven to 350°F. Peel and slice your apples and then sprinkle with the lemon juice so that they don't turn brown. Set the apples aside. Add salt to the flour and mix well. Cut one stick of butter into flour and add hot water. When the consistency is such that it all sticks together, form the dough into a ball and roll it out on a pastry cloth. Remember, the harder you work it, the tougher it'll be, so don't overwork the dough.

So, let's say you're making individual tarts, rather that one big one. In that case, you cut pieces of pastry about the size of a child's hand into a triangle or a square, put the apple slices in the middle with a generous shaving of butter from your second stick. Cover

the top of the apple and butter with a thick sprinkling
of sugar and grate fresh nutmeg all around. Fold up
the sides but do not pinch closed. Bake twenty-five to
thirty minutes. Remove from oven, let cool, and enjoy.

✺ Seems to me like making sugar cookies with my grandmother was as much fun as starting the first hyacinth or paper
white bulbs in the fall. She had bunches of cookie cutters—
moons, stars, angels, and gingerbread men. And when it came
cookie-making time, it was also always time to make popcorn
strings and colored paper chains for the Christmas tree. She
didn't believe in store-bought trees, in fact, even if you found a
tree in the woods that was as perfectly shaped as one from a
tree lot, she'd still opt for the scraggliest, most pitiful seedling
that she could find. We'd go tree hunting in the woods behind
her house (which are now subdivision woods) and pilfer with
no discretion whatsoever. Even in the last ten years, she
wouldn't believe that *she* had to ask to go into *her* old woods
and would drag her descendants after her to cut trees near tennis courts and tidy subdivision entrances. But once we got the
tree, she'd be ready to start decorating with sugar cookies,
popcorn strings, and colored paper chains, the instructions for
which follow below.

✺ SUGAR COOKIES, POPCORN STRINGS, AND COLORED PAPER CHAINS

cookie ingredients
1-1/2 cups confectioners sugar
1 cup butter
1 egg

1 teaspoon vanilla extract
2-1/2 cups all-purpose flour
1 teaspoon baking soda
1 teaspoon cream of tartar
Sugar sprinkles

Cream sugar and butter and then add egg and vanilla
and mix well. In another bowl, mix dry ingredients
and then blend it all into the butter mixture. Put
dough in the refrigerator for two to three hours.

Preheat oven to 375°F. Divide dough in half and roll
out thin on pastry cloth covered with flour. Decorate
the cookies with sugar sprinkles or any way you like—
try a few yourself but remember the cutest ones will be
the ones the children in your party make. They may
not all be the baby Jesus or Santa Claus, in fact a few
may be submachine guns or race cars, but they will be
original and they'll be completely at home on your
scraggly tree.

popcorn strings ingredients:
Plain popcorn
2 to 3 spools heavy thread
Package of big-eyed needles

Pop the popcorn, thread a needle, and begin to string
the kernels one by one. That easy? Not quite.
Remember, to a child, perhaps even to you, stringing
popcorn is a long and arduous task and it can prove
painful, though not fatal, to fingers. For this reason,
don't make each person's thread too long. When everyone has had enough, tie the different lengths together
and wrap it around just the front of the tree.

colored paper chain ingredients:
2 to 3 big packages of colored construction paper
Scissors
Paste or glue

for the workers:
1 to 2 children (before they reach adolescence)
2 to 3 clean aprons
Energy

Paper chain-making goes on at the kitchen table while the baking goes on around the stove and the chopping block. I like paper chains and think they make the holiday season.

My grandmother liked simple items on her little tree and was a naysayer to electric lights. It was her strong desire that her Christmas tree have real white candles, whether she burned down her cabin or not. Me and my brother always wanted colored lights that bubbled. She'd give in for white lights that didn't bubble but had a problem with the other kind. It wasn't until Jack persuaded her that she finally bought us the most beautiful set of bubbling lights. Thanks, Jack.

Cut lengths of construction paper about eight-inches long and two-inches wide. Paste the ends of one strip together making a loop. Next, loop the next link into the first as if making a necklace. Continue until you have enough length to decorate your tree. Paper chains are festive not only on the Christmas tree, but also as garlands of color decorating doorways and staircases.

Keep the children overnight and take them to
church the next morning. They'll be sweet little sleepy-
heads. If you have a copy of *Christmas in Georgia* by
Celestine Sibley, read it to them by the fire before you
put them to bed.

❦ I include instructions for the following project because
making gumdrop trees is such a vivid memory for me and they
are probably something a lot of folks grew up with. Gumdrop
trees must have become popular during the time when penny
or hard candy was in vogue. Having much less selection when
the world was much smaller, there must have been a fairy-tale
quality to a tree that grew gumdrops—the sugar sparkling on
the white branches, chewy candy there for the picking.

❦ GUMDROP TREE

Branch with lots of limbs
Can of white spray paint
Bucket with enough rocks, sand, or dirt to stabilize the
    branch
Napkin to tie around the base of the limb to hide rocks
    and dirt
 Big bag of small gumdrops

Spraypaint the tree limb outside and allow time to dry.
Stick it in your dirt bucket but don't expect it to stand
straight up—they never do. Tie the napkin around the
base of the limb. Let your children stick the gumdrops
on each branch. Place in a high-traffic area. Refertilize
with gumdrops as needed.

CHAPTER NINE

A couple of weeks before Christmas 1998, my grandmother mentioned casually over the telephone that she had a doctor's appointment for a bone scan at Piedmont Hospital.

"You want company?" I asked, then added half-jokingly, "Someone to hold your hand?"

"That'd be fine," she said, I imagine from the rocking chair in her kitchen where she sat drinking coffee in the early morning hours and talking on the black wall phone. "I'll go to the office and write a column and then I'll pick you up."

Her habit of picking me up was twofold: one, at that point, she was out of her Hollywood junker car phase and into vehicles that were nice, tankish, easy to drive and reliable; and two, she could check on the progress of the renovation of our house in East Point.

She'd been complaining about headaches and a bum leg that was giving her trouble when she walked. She'd been to a neurologist for the headaches and had been diagnosed with neuralgia. As for her leg, at the island she'd taken a fall into a boat and assumed that her leg was aching because of that. But months of treatment had gone on, all to no avail. Finally, she called Dr. Martin York, the Atlanta oncologist who'd treated her breast cancer back in 1995. I figured he scheduled the bone scan to be on the safe side.

The equipment in the hospital for MRIs is a long, space age-looking tube in which one lays. My grandmother was locked into this metal thing and a computer screen showed the intimate picture of her skeleton, more invasive to view than seeing someone stark naked. I asked the technician what all the white spots on the image meant. The reply, I'm sure the one received by many a nosy family member, was that he couldn't tell us. The pictures would have to be studied, diagnosed, and then passed onto her oncologist for prognosis.

When they were finished scanning and had gotten all the pictures they wanted, 'Tine and I asked if we could wait outside for the results. She was anxious, more agitated that I expected her to be. And because of that, it began slowly to dawn on me that she was truly scared that something was wrong.

"What if it *is* something?" I asked. "You gonna be okay with that?"

"Why shouldn't I be?" she snapped. "I've had a full long life. I've been happy. I don't have to live forever—I just want to know what's wrong with me. If I'm not going to feel any better, I might as well go. Everyone has their time, it's natural."

She was angry, not at me, but at the situation. I stepped lightly with my words. Problem with that, is you make light of something very serious, you appear as if you don't care.

And then if you worry out loud, you're making it worse for the person getting the news.

She got up to walk down the hall and I rose to help her—as inconspicuously as possible, just being there in case she needed my arm in a pinch. I tried to slip my hand under her arm and she flinched.

"I don't need any help, thank you," she said. "I need results."

I put myself to some use and began worrying the technicians about how she'd sleep easier if she could get an answer right away. They felt for us but ultimately sent us away empty-handed.

The walk to the parking deck was brutally silent. There was nothing for me to say and my grandmother was deep in dark thoughts. We had just made the car when one of the technicians caught up with us, a big orange x-ray envelope in his hands. "Miss Sibley? Dr. York wants you to come up to his office right away—take this with you," he told us with some urgency. It was pointless to ask him what we were facing though something told us he *knew*.

"Doesn't sound good," 'Tine said, willing her feet not to stumble, taking my arm, eyes turned upwards to the huge building as if towards a scaffold.

"It may be fine," I offered weakly. "You never know what he's gonna tell us."

"That's right," she agreed, angrier than ever at my pat and pathetic explanation, "*you never know*."

Dr. York did not keep us waiting long. When he came into the exam room, he sat down, asked the perfunctory questions about how she was doing, and then he got down to the truth. There were tears in his eyes as he told her the cancer had returned and it was terminal, that there was nothing to be done. The cancer had spread all through her bones and other tests would have to be performed to see where else. She took the news calmly and, as I looked at her practical stoic face, I felt tears rushing down my hot cheeks, a torrent of sadness that was unstoppable.

"There, there's my good child," she stopped thinking of herself and put her arm around me. "It's okay. It ain't the worst thing that could happen—"

"It's just . . . I don't want *this* to happen," I said, trying to turn myself around, to be strong, to get rid of those damned tears.

When the moment passed, she turned back to business. "How long?" she willed the words to come out.

Everyone who's been through a cancer knows *they* have no idea *how long*. It could be a couple of months and it could be it never gets you at all. Dr. York knew my grandmother and her wishes like a priest knows his confessor. He'd gotten her through the first cancer—the hideous bouts in the chemo room, the weakness, and the slow uncertain recovery. But Dr. York knew that this cancer had gone so far, he had enough respect not to suggest worthless measures that would drain the quality out of what little life she had left.

"Of course there are new medicines that could help manage the pain and slow it down but there's really nothing we can do . . . ," he said.

But she was cheerful, even though it was as if a firefighter was standing there telling her that her house had just burned down and she was saying, "It's okay—you can't save them all."

What goes through a person's mind at a moment like that? Our visit over, she went to talk to Lynn, Dr. York's assistant. I was so overwhelmed by the news, I just wanted to curl up in a corner and turn my brain off. I couldn't stop the tears and so while she was talking I ducked into a back room and tried to let some of it out. A kind young woman, maybe a nurse, followed me into the dark room and put her arms around me.

"Are you okay?" she asked.

"No," I said. "I'm not. Do you know what news I just got?"

She nodded. The word had spread around the office like a bad virus.

"I know I'm not supposed to be crying. Why is that? It's horrible. She's my grandmother—you don't understand—it was just her and me and the boys for so long. I just can't picture life without her." I was saying all of this to a complete stranger.

"We're all broken up about it," she said, by then just patting my arm, helplessly. "Your grandmother is very well loved."

Me and 'Tine left Dr. York's office, stunned, numb, unconscious of breathing. She said she'd just spend the night in town with us after we stopped at her favorite barbecue place and got a sandwich. She needed some time to process the information before she dealt with the whole clan.

But as I was pulling out of the hospital's garage onto Peachtree Street, I started tearing up again.

"What's wrong with you?" she asked. "Do you want me to drive?"

"No, I don't want you to drive. Excuse me, but I am upset. This is very upsetting. I don't want to lose you," I said.

Why is it that important moments have to be borne with stoicism? Why couldn't we just talk through it until it went away? She was having none of that—she was in no mood to cry over her misfortune—she was mad as hell.

We got to the barbecue place and went inside to eat, ordering more to take home to the boys and Ron. I decided to stop with the questions and with the free offering of misery and let her talk and ask the questions she wanted answered. She ate a sandwich and a cup of Brunswick stew, her standard order. Nothing tasted good to me.

In the parking lot, after we paid and tipped the waitress, she asked, "You saw the pictures. Could you tell how much there was and where it was?"

I could. But the question was, being very bad with such situations, was I supposed to tell her? She always said I was the one who answered her honestly, but I think she said that to a lot of us whenever she was truth seeking. I thought a moment and then I decided, *I'd* sure wanna know. I began pointing to the corresponding places on my own body as I remembered each spot. By the time I was finished it was plain that she was lit up like a Christmas tree.

She was interested in these details, marveling that her body could have come to such a state behind her back, without her knowing. We drove home in silence.

Ron met us on the porch. As the boys ran up to mob 'Tine, their usual hugging and offering to tote her overnight luggage, Ron followed me back to the kitchen where I spilled more tears.

"She's not dead yet. This is not the time to grieve," he rebuked me. "You have to be strong for her—there'll be plenty of time to grieve later."

Knowing that Ron's father had played much the same role in his life as 'Tine had in mine and that Ron had nursed his father for six months before losing him to cancer, I asked just what it was that he had done to combat his own feelings.

"There was too much to do to worry about it," he said, holding me. I dried my tears on his shirt, took a deep breath and returned, fortified, and, I hoped, useful.

Ron came out of the kitchen and, as 'Tine came down the hall saying, "I guess she told you—," he wrapped his arms around her and told her he was sorry, that we all loved her. He was so calm, so knowing of the right words and actions.

We hadn't done much Christmas shopping but, it turned out, we had already bought 'Tine's present. It was a good time to break the family rules about early gift-opening, one, because surprises can take you away from yourself for a moment; and two, because the present was a warm pair of flannel pajamas that she could wear right away.

It had been such an exhausting day, one of the most exhausting of my life. She walked back to Wolfie's room where she slept in his bed, a bed with four acorn posts that sat so high off the ground that it looked like a Mardi Gras float. She liked to sleep there because she'd bought the bed herself years ago at a Salvation Army thrift store. We put a fresh bulb in the bedside lamp so she could read and I scanned the bookshelves around the house for books that she hadn't yet pilfered.

When my grandmother emerged from her second great-grandson's room, she was wearing her new Christmas pajamas. We were outside hovering and greeted her like a pack of wolves. To show off, she lifted her legs and danced a funny jig, turning round and round with her hands up testifying so we could all see how good her nightclothes fit.

Once she was settled, I went in with an armload of books. "You need anything else?" I asked.

"I was thinking maybe I should call your mother and tell her and then maybe *you* should call everyone else," she said.

I was in my useful phase when I agreed.

Did I mention? I am not good at taking bad news, much less at spreading it. I take no pleasure in being "the one"—I'd much rather a big brother do the dirty work. I'm notorious for calling Bird and putting such jobs off on him. In fact, when 'Tine had gone in the hospital for heart surgery in 1997 and decided not to tell anyone *but* me, I broke my vow of silence and made Bird come down to the hospital to wait it out with me. Oh, yeah, and tell everyone else.

But it wasn't enough that I call. Some people I just couldn't bring myself to contact and I'd piggyback one call on another by telling the news to one person myself and asking that person to pass it on. After each call was made, after I had let the grim reaper into the lives of so many people she loved, 'Tine wanted a report.

What I mean by report is that 'Tine wanted to know how each and every person had reacted to her news, if they'd been alright, if they'd been sorry enough. When the deed was done, she went to bed, read a little, and fell fast asleep.

I, on the other hand, cried myself awake every time my eyelids got heavy. Now, what kind of person was I to depend on?

This was all before Christmas and no one was decided as how best to celebrate the holiday. But I knew that 'Tine wanted to spend her last Christmas Eve night with us in East Point, to see what Santa Claus would bring the boys. She wanted me to put up greenery on the mantelpiece and arrange furniture just so. The fireplace didn't work but that didn't mean skimping on magnolia leaves to decorate it. At K-mart she insisted we purchase a plastic nativity scene to replace the ceramic one that had been broken in the move. She brought some of her old Christmas ornaments—scratched bulbs, an old Santa—and she decorated the place up nice, proving that peeling plaster in no way prohibits making a house warm and inviting. I did everything she told me.

On Christmas day, the whole clan gathered at Sweet Apple, putting differences aside and, after we ate, we all stood around the old organ while my little sister Betsy played and we sang

"Silent Night." Did 'Tine guess some of her descendants felt out-of-place singing the old hymn? If she did, it didn't matter. She stood in the middle of us, crooning high above the crowd, the very loudest, "Round yon Virgin, mother and child! Holy infant, so tender and mild!"

What followed just after the holidays was more testing. By then, the whole bunch of us was one big worried mess. We tagged along like a herd to her doctors' appointments, taking up the halls and the empty chairs of waiting rooms, bothering doctors and nurses as if 'Tine were the only patient.

We all went to those things so much that it got to be a sort of regular meeting. We were waiting for her to get her first round of scans after the diagnosis when I caught up with her by the elevator. She was late because she'd been at her office and frankly, she was having too much fun to leave.

"Hey granny," I said cheerfully, giving her one of my half hugs. "You look like you're in good spirits."

"You know what I've decided?" she asked with the look of a child who fears she may be asking too much. "I've decided I like life. When I'm at the office, I really have fun. I've decided I'm not ready to die—I have too much to do still."

"Well, you know what Dr. York said about the new medication. You want me to call him and tell him you wanna make an effort?"

"Yes," she whispered.

It wasn't easy though. All that stiff-upper-lip stuff doesn't mean a lot to me. When I looked around, I may have seen bravery, but even bravery doesn't hide the truth. We were a family in fear. The most I could get out of my grandmother was her view of heaven. She said the best way for me to accept

187

what was happening was to be grateful for the time we'd had together—that's what she had done in the past. She said she thought heaven was a place filled with all of the people she had loved, who had gone before her—people like Muv and my grandfather and Jack. The one thing she couldn't quite figure out, she said, was if you'd been married more than once, which husband you would be with. Everyone figured it'd be Jack but then, you never know.

I don't know why she decided that I should be granted her power of attorney. At first, no one thought it was a good decision—many in the family believed in the old-fashioned ideal of a male shouldering the burden. I couldn't have agreed more fully.

But there it was. Be strong. Be useful and responsible. I accepted on the grounds that her accountant Tom Downs and her money manager Curtis Hedrick help me through the job by advising and giving what I knew would be sound counsel. I had no experience of my own from which to draw.

But 'Tine wouldn't be talked out of it. She enjoyed my discomfort to no end and started calling me the "P of A" like I was a royal court manager of some kind. I wasn't. Any *Ask Sibley*s that came my way, I turned around and asked Mr. Downs and Mr. Hedrick.

My grandmother loved driving or, as she called it, "kiting around Atlanta." She would point out former crime sites where she'd all but solved the murders herself: a daughter-in-law who was stabbed and stuffed in a trunk in a basement until the foul-smelling body was discovered when it floated from the trunk during a flood; the restaurant lady down in Macon who'd poisoned her children, parents, and husbands for the insurance money (my grandmother still took her the banana she requested from prison). 'Tine talked about giving up her job but she just kept working. She kept kiting around

Atlanta and working in spite of the disease quietly and per-sistently invading her body.

I began worrying about her making the thirty-mile drive to work every day in traffic. I was trying to figure out ways to keep her out of the car—like pushing the seat back so she couldn't reach the wheel. One day I simply went home with her and took her car and told her I needed it. I got her a ride ready for the next day but it was too late. She went to the car rental place and got her own wheels. And then she called me a "frustrated dictator."

January went by and then February and March. There was no change in 'Tine's condition. She took her treatments and she lived as if nothing was wrong. Things seemed so strangely normal that it was an easy idea to fall into. It was easy because we wanted to believe it. She was still talking about finishing her final novel, *Green Trees Abending*, a sequel to *Jincey* based in her childhood. I thought the sequel was her best work. When I read the first fifty manuscript pages I saw her as the brilliant writer she was, not just as my grandmother. By April, she needed a break and decided to go to Dog Island to work on the book. She planned a month's vacation.

Then, one morning in May of 1999, my phone rang. I missed it. The message on our machine was "Sibley? This is 'Tine. I'm just calling to say that I haven't talked to you in *for-ever*." I called my grandmother back. She'd been on vacation and a record week had passed without a word between us.

"Where have you been, child?" she asked, hearing my voice.

"Here," I said firmly. "Where have you been?"

"I've been here," she said. "Well, here with company. They just left. What's been going on with you?"

"Well, my mother-in-law Luvenia came and I had a big deadline . . . ," I began. My mother-in-law had come but there had been more before that. Workers had come to fix the sill on the front porch, a process that required reinforcing the whole front of the house. They worked nearly until midnight and one early morning, they came back and roused me from sleep. When I went into the kitchen to make coffee, the floor shook like an earthquake under my feet. They were replacing the sill that held up the back kitchen wall.

"The porch got fixed this week," I added after reflection. "And Wolfie had poison ivy and stayed home for two days— I guess that was early in the week . . ."

"You have had a busy week," said my grandmother before lowering her tone to ominous and foreboding. "How did the mother-in-law visit go?"

"Oh, that. Fine. I like her a lot. She reminds me of you. I told her that and she said, 'I've always liked to think I was like myself'—just like you do, 'Tine," I said.

There was a silence on the line. "Well that's awful then. Just like me—we wouldn't want that, would we?"

I changed the subject. "Vincent had spend-the-night company and we took them to Six Flags—that was the day after we drove my mother-in-law back to Birmingham. She slept in your bed."

"Wolfie's bed?"

"Yep. I bought some new sheets and they're a light blue cotton. I didn't get white because, well, it is Wolfie. He took one disdainful look at the color and said, 'Now who would have that color blue on their bed?'"

Getting a bed together for a mother-in-law also included new pillows, a summer blanket, and a cleaning effort tantamount to sweeping away the rubble of a small bombed village. When Luvenia arrived, the dishes were piled high in the sink—I'd only had time to haul away the rotten porch rafters left by the construction crew, get Vincent to mow the yard, and push the laundry to one side of the hallway so there was a path to the good bathroom.

"Oh, and there wasn't a door on Wolfie's room so Ron had to hang one. And there also wasn't a door on the boy's bathroom because Ron had gutted the room and it's really only a toilet at the moment and Ron had to go looking for the door that went to it and hang that one, too.

"But," I continued, "I'm looking out the window and my morning glories and moon flowers and sunflower seeds which I planted at the beginning of the month have come up! No word on the lavender. Four packets of seeds, fertilizer—I was as careful as I knew how to be, and nothing. I beginning to wonder if lavender even comes from seeds."

"I'm pretty sure it does," my grandmother said wryly, not finding humor in my dilemma. "I'll stop by a nursery on the way home and get you a couple of plants."

"And then when I dropped the boys off for school this morning, before Wolfie got out of the car, he heaved a long sigh and said, 'Boy, I sure hope today is Friday.'"

"What did you tell him?" my grandmother asked.

"Nope, Wolf. It's only Monday."

※ I forgot to wish 'Tine a happy eighty-fifth birthday, May 23, 1999—that's the sort of thing you start thinking about when you lose someone. She was at the island and I know we talked, but I missed saying the words. When she got back to Sweet Apple, she wanted her present to be a trip to Holly Creek with a picnic on the porch there. I promised we'd go but then never got around to it. There was all of this P of A stuff to do and I'd taken on a couple of small jobs.

※ On what was to prove to be our last trip together—to Louisville, Kentucky, to accept the Lifetime Achievement Award from the National Society of Newspaper Columnists in June, 1999—'Tine and I had an all-night pajama party with her two favorite editors from the *AJC*, Amanda Miller and Eileen Drennen. We were talking over our party clothes for her big award the next day, pulling out shoes, matching scarves. 'Tine produced a white dress from her hanging bag, one we'd bought together at Greenbriar Mall near Atlanta.

Amanda, who'd edited a column by 'Tine about how expensive the dress was and how 'Tine had had me return it, gasped, "Isn't that the dress in your column?"

"Amanda," I broke in before my grandmother could answer, "there's something you need to understand. Column life doesn't always run parallel to real life. And I bet all those newspaper people are going to be talking about ethics stuff tomorrow."

I am not a journalist, not really. But my grandmother was a reporter first, and an author second. She considered reporting the highest calling and I'll hazard a guess that Amanda and Eileen felt the same way. The next morning at breakfast, Eileen quoted me with some alarm—"ethics stuff."

'Tine never tired of embarrassing me. Especially in a crowd, she'd enjoy watching me squirm, saying to a freelance writer in a loud, carrying voice, "Don't you know of a job for Sibley? She needs a job!" Or passing a help-wanted sign at a convenience store or hamburger stand, she'd say, "Don't you need a job, honey? They're hiring there. I bet they'd hire you if you applied."

I can't be sure what was going on in her mind when she did this. But when I think back, it was probably for two reasons, first, she believed no one had a right to say they were a writer unless they were getting paid for it; and second, that no one had a right to say they were working unless they were employed full-time. Freelance, in her book, was just another word for nothing left to loose. This was one of our subjects of debate.

The trip to Louisville functioned more than an award-getting, getting-out-of-town jaunt. When the committee approached her, it had been a distant and future date, nailed down around December for the following June, a period of six months. Once she'd agreed, it meant that it was another six months she'd have to be around to show up to accept the award. The minute she got home from Louisville, she started planning a house party for all of her friends. She showed me the list. Everyone who had meant anything to her, even those long out of touch, were invited to a gala gathering at Sweet Apple in August.

Her routine didn't change. She continued to get up every morning and to say her prayers. She had a lot of people she was praying for and she kept track of them all in the form of an invisible tree. One limb would be one branch of the family with the smaller branches representing children. She had an order that she would sometimes explain. Looking into thin air, she saw the faces of the people she was talking to God about. 'Tine was interested in all of us having a spiritual life but beyond giving us each a copy of *Daily Strengths for Daily Needs* by Mary W. Tileston, (published in 1884), she tried to hang back and let us develop our own relationships to God.

I have been accused by a number of my kinfolk of being a worrier, in fact, of enjoying the process. I did not enjoy, however, the day I couldn't find my grandmother in her office and found her at home instead. She was groggy on the phone and told me she'd fallen and hit her nose and had climbed back into her bed to sleep it off.

The males in our family don't much like to indulge me when I worry but when I called my cousin, John Bazemore, who lives ten minutes away from Sweet Apple and asked him to look in at 'Tine, he did. He looked in on her as she was staring up at the bathroom ceiling and he said he quickly helped her up—before she could notice that the ceiling needed painting.

Although my cousin assured me 'Tine was all right, I drove out to the country *just to be sure.* And there's a lot of *just being sure* involved in a worrier's life. Of course, I thought maybe she'd hit her head and an x-ray would tell more. While I was rousing her from her bed, my mother called. "Wanna come to the ER with us?" I asked.

Turned out Mom had had a light stroke the night before. I drove the two of them to Piedmont Hospital along with my mother's husband. While her doctors let my grandmother go, they kept my mother and she remained in the hospital over a week.

That was the beginning of the end for 'Tine. The true beginning, the signs that were indisputable, that could not be ignored or explained away, though even at that point, I think I tried. No sooner was my mother out of the hospital than the next day, my little brother David called and asked me to meet him and my mother back at Piedmont Hospital. 'Tine had fallen, he said, but there was no time to explain beyond that.

I'm pretty certain we were all present, all the seeming millions of children and grandchildren. We were holding each other up as my grandmother lay unconscious in the emergency room.

She'd had another stroke and she remained unconscious for the next few days. We took turns sitting by her bed, putting socks on her feet, which were always so cold. We talked to each other in hushed tones outside her room and never left her alone.

The doctors thought we'd be lucky to get her home one last time and cautioned that she might not come to again. I reached back deep in my memory to try to get the last words I had said to her, the last words she had spoken to me when I'd left her the day before propped up on pillows on the porch swing. Did I say *I love you?* Did she say, *Come back when you can?* I wasn't sure.

I reasoned the way I thought she would reason. This was not a quality of life that was acceptable to her—this semi-comatose state—so let the angels take her, I said to myself. I got a copy of her living will and kept it by her bed should a meddling doctor or nurse try to go against her wishes.

Then one afternoon, as I was fixing her blanket, getting ready to hand over to the next shift, out of the blue she said, "God bless my good child."

The next day, she came back to us as if nothing had happened and she was mad as hell at me. She wasn't going to have any caregiver, no chance that she'd stop driving. She was going to go where she wanted, when she wanted, and that was that.

"Do you know that we thought you were a goner?" I asked, though I know she'd already repeatedly been told. "We thought we'd be lucky to get you home to die. Now you have to follow doctor's orders and recover before you go anywhere."

God only knows how mad she got at me. I didn't like confronting my grandmother, arguing, insisting. I hated it. My cousin John confided to me that he felt I was her whipping boy. But, he added, he and my brother Bird were proud of me for my hanging in there and doing what was right. If I needed to talk, they'd both be there to listen.

But Curtis Hedrick, money manager and problem solver, helped out. He knew a wonderful woman, Carol DeVaney, who was some sort of an angel, a real angel. She was the gentlest, most capable soul when it came to taking care of the reluctant sick and she happened also to be a fan of my grandmother. It was a day or so before 'Tine caught on that Carol was there all the time. 'Tine took to calling her her "tenant lady."

It all happened so fast. Basically, we got Carol, then we got 'Tine home only to discover it wasn't heart problems, it was the cancer in her brain that had knocked her out. Within hours, that news was followed by a move to hospice care. There was no point in making her stay anywhere for medical treatment. She wanted to go to Muv's house in Alford and to Holley where she herself had been born. And she wanted to go right away. But it wasn't that easy—there were logistics to consider. I went out to the country to check on her and she was less than happy to see me.

"What's going on?" I asked, coming around the corner from the top of the stairs.

She had a stubborn look on her face. "I don't know. You tell. Everyone says 'Ask Sibley, ask Sibley.' I want to go to Alford, so I'm asking *you*, can I go?"

My uncle Jimmy and his wife Peggy had lived in Muv's house for years. She wanted to see her son, to get away from all the prying eyes and bed hoverers, myself included.

I pulled up a chair beside her bed and let out a tired sigh. "'Tine you can do anything you want to do."

"Then I'm leaving for Alford today, as soon as I can get packed up," she informed me.

I hated it. She couldn't go without Carol—doctor's orders— and I had to be the bad guy and duke it out with my grandmother. Fortunately, my big brother Bird came up the stairs not too long into our argument—John and he were going to drive her and Carol to Alford the next day. They were my saving grace—there weren't too many things she loved more than being with her two eldest grandsons, John and Bird.

So they left and we didn't talk much while she was gone. I called every day to talk to Carol or my uncle, to make sure 'Tine was hanging in there. She was distant, angry. Rumors were flying around about how she'd gone to Alford to die in Muv's bed—all the signs were there. She made her trip to Holley not even getting out of the car at the cemetery to see Grandpa's grave. Then, a little over a week later, she was ready to make a trip to Dog Island.

Carol DeVaney had not had a break, not one, in many weeks. But, she assured me, she was in it for the long haul—whatever my grandmother wanted to do, she would be there to help her do it and make her comfortable along the way.

At the island, family started pouring in—two by two and four by four. She loved seeing each and every one of her children—her grandchildren, their husbands and wives. I kept thinking I should go and she kept asking when I would.

❧ Debra Childers, her assistant at the paper for several years, flew down with a thousand letters from her readers. Debra called me and told me in no uncertain terms that I needed to drop what I was doing and make haste.

I was indecisive at best. I was suddenly busy. I didn't want to remember her as sick and frail. I didn't have any unresolved issues. I'd had more time with 'Tine in the last years than anyone else—best to give the others in the family these final fleeting moments.

Obligations began to fall out of trees. But then something struck me—I wanted to see her face. The reports were grim and, worst of all, she sounded weak and she'd stop asking when I'd be there.

I didn't want to say good-bye to my grandmother. I figured maybe if I avoided sending her off, it would stop the inevitable. But then on Friday the thirteenth of August, I found myself getting up at four in the morning, packing up the car with my little brother John-Stephen in tow, and making the six-hour drive to Dog Island where 'Tine was laid up in bed giving last instructions to everyone in the family—everyone save me. When I walked into her bedroom I knew immediately why I'd come.

She stretched out her arms big and a smile like pure joy set over her face as she exclaimed, "Tibo! I'd thought I'd never see you again!"

"I thought I'd never see *you* again," I finally admitted as I put my arms around her thin shoulders and squeezed her as hard as I dared. I sat in the rocking chair beside her bed, holding her hand until she fell asleep and then I cried. My mother came in, touched my arm, and reminded me it was probably best not to let her see me crying.

That night I slept with 'Tine the last time, in Carol's bed next to hers. I promised Carol that I'd come get her if my grandmother woke for anything.

Is she really dying? That was the thought that went through my head. She was so strong, always—I wouldn't have been surprised if she'd beaten the cancer like she had so many other threats to her life. No one knew for sure if she would—only God.

Carol was good. She seemed to sense something that can't be seen by looking at blood work or feeling a pulse. "I think it's soon," she told me in a quiet moment on the porch.

She said I might go ahead and say anything I wanted to. I thought about it. Every time 'Tine and I had gotten in a fight, we'd made up. Our long talks on the road to book signings had provided a perfect venue to hash over old childhood worries and fears. What did I have to say at that point? Then it hit me: *Thank you.*

Do you remember that game you taught me and how we made fairy rooms in the roots of trees? An acorn would be a cap, a leaf a bed, a stick a person, moss would be carpet—do you remember that, 'Tine?

❧ The next day, a Saturday, my husband, a great cook, flew down and with him came the familiar smells of blueberry pancakes, baked ham, and crabs fresh from the bay. The teenage boys in our family swept the sand off the porch and a warm salt breeze blew foreboding whispers through the house. The dogs were uneasy, nervous.

Close to five in the morning, I woke up of a sudden impulse, a noise, a groan. I rubbed the sleep from my eyes and headed towards my grandmother's room. Her "tenant lady" was busy tending her, trying to make her comfortable. The pain from the cancer had seeped through the medicine and was torturing what she called her "unfriendly bones."

I sat beside her bed and said the words that I imagine people have said since the beginning of time. "I'm here. We all love you so much. Everybody has a job. Everything is taken care of. It's okay to let go. . . ."

My mother sat down by me and softly sang age-old tunes that sounded like lullabies. We held 'Tine's hands as she gazed back and forth between this world and the next, the pain finally gone. And then just as in a church, as in a poem or a piece of wisdom, her spirit slipped from her body as quietly as it had been conceived.

I called Ellen, and asked her to pick up Vincent and Wolfie, give them the news, wipe away tears, reassure. Ellen has been like an aunt to the boys ever since she came into our lives. Ellen and her husband Rodney took the boys out for pizza and explained.

"But 'Tine's not supposed to die!" Wolfie sobbed.

🦋 When we got back home the next day I was walking through the house, coffee in hand, and remembering. Then I came upon Wolfie in the music room, a wrinkled letter protected under his small hand.

All I could see was the outside. It read:

> *Address: heaven*
> *From: Wolfie*

His eyes were swollen red, the tears spilling off his long lashes in currents of grief.

I gently pried the note from his protective custody and my tears welled up as I read the childish handwritten words:

> *Tein I miss you very much and I wish you were here. I hope you see everybody in heaven and when I come I will see you. I wonder what is like there and I could be with you but it will just half to be your spearot until I get there. But when I do we will have lots of fun and we can run on the clouds and fly. And we can do anything we want me you my mom and ron and betsy and my brother. I hope you get this leter love Wolfie.*

And, as he folded it shut and put down his pen, I knew she had.

Fare-thee-well, dear heart—
A fine fare-thee-well

ACKNOWLEDGMENTS

I 'd like to thank the following people for hanging in there and being supportive while this humble book was written: my husband Ron Letcher and sons Vincent and Wolfie Schaum for living without me being "all there" for a while; my big brother Charles "Bird" Fleming for picking up the phone at 6:00 A.M. on a Saturday morning and for brotherly advice (whether I took it or not); thanks to my mother Mary Vance for understanding; all of 'Tine's grandchildren and great-grandchildren who loved her and let me share her; blessings on publisher Tom Payton for his encouragement and inspiration; gratitude and thanks to my wonderful editor Patrick Allen for all of his hard work; love to Debra Childers for just being Debra; many warm thanks to Susan Soper who was so good to my granny; to all of the folks at the *Atlanta Journal-Constitution* who knew and loved Celestine Sibley and who let that love pass on to her family in time of need; cheers and thanks to murder mystery writer and friend Kathy Hogan Trocheck for her mentoring; and lastly, thank you to Ellen Howle and Rodney Ho for letting me plop my laptop on their coffee table from time to time.